LAWS AND PROGRAMS

WORKERS' COMPENSATION INSURANCE

A PRIMER

LAWS AND PROGRAMS

Additional books in this series can be found on Nova's website under the Series tab.

Additional E-books in this series can be found on Nova's website under the E-book tab.

LAWS AND PROGRAMS

WORKERS' COMPENSATION INSURANCE

A PRIMER

EMMANUEL SANFORD
EDITOR

NOVINKA
New York

For permission to use material from this book please contact us:
Telephone 631-231-7269; Fax 631-231-8175
Web Site: http://www.novapublishers.com

Additional color graphics may be available in the e-book version of this book.

Library of Congress Cataloging-in-Publication Data

ISBN: 978-1-63117-651-7

Published by Nova Science Publishers, Inc. † New York

CONTENTS

PREFACE

Workers' compensation insurance covers nearly all workers in the U.S. and provides those who are injured or become ill as a result of work with medical treatment, a portion of lost wages, and a lump sum for some permanent impairments. Nonetheless, there are limitations to conducting studies that rely on workers' compensation records since not all injuries and illnesses result in claims being filed. Furthermore, the data that are collected are not readily combined if obtained from multiple sources since requirements vary substantially among the states. This book was written to help describe elements of the workers' compensation insurance programs in the U.S. and the potential to utilize the records for public health purposes. This book also focuses on several key policy issues facing the program, including the disproportionate share of claims and program costs attributed to postal workers, the payment of FECA benefits after retirement age, the overall level of FECA disability benefits as compared with those offered by the states, and the administration of the FECA program.

Chapter 1 – Occupational safety and health research and surveillance are essential for the prevention and control of injuries, illnesses and hazards that arise from the workplace. Research and surveillance can fill gaps in knowledge about where hazards exist and what interventions are effective at preventing workplace injuries, illnesses and fatalities. Workers' compensation insurance records are a resource used for these primary prevention purposes. In addition, workers' compensation records may be used for early detection of health outcomes in populations of workers which is part of secondary prevention. They may also be used to help identify effective medical treatment which is part of tertiary prevention. Workers' compensation insurance covers nearly all workers in the U.S. and provides those who are injured or become ill as a result of work with medical treatment, a portion of lost wages, and a lump sum for some permanent impairments. Nonetheless, there are limitations to conducting studies that rely on workers' compensation records since not all injuries and illnesses result in claims being filed. Furthermore, the data that are collected are not readily combined if obtained from multiple sources since requirements vary substantially among the states. The National Institute for Occupational Safety and Health (NIOSH) joined with a number of public and private sector co-sponsors to convene two workshops on the use of workers' compensation data for occupational safety and health. Creation of this document was suggested at the second workshop as a means to describe elements of the workers' compensation insurance programs in the U.S. and the potential to utilize the records for public health purposes. Public health agencies, the workers' compensation industry, trade associations and the state-level programs share interests in utilizing these data to protect workers from occupational injuries and illnesses. To help facilitate these goals, NIOSH has created a Center for Workers' Compensation Studies. Further information on the center may be obtained at http://www.cdc.gov /niosh/topics/ workerComp/CWCS/.

Chapter 2 – The Federal Employees' Compensation Act (FECA) is the workers' compensation program for federal employees. Like all workers' compensation programs, FECA pays disability, survivors, and medical benefits, without fault, to employees who are injured or become ill in the course of their federal employment and the survivors of employees killed on the job. The FECA program is administered by the Department of Labor (DOL) and the costs of benefits are paid by each employee's host agency. Employees of the U.S. Postal Service (USPS) currently comprise the largest group of FECA beneficiaries and are responsible for the largest share of FECA benefits.

In: Workers' Compensation Insurance
Editor: Emmanuel Sanford

ISBN: 978-1-63117-651-7

Chapter 1

WORKERS' COMPENSATION INSURANCE: A PRIMER FOR PUBLIC HEALTH*

David F. Utterback,
Alysha R. Meyers and Steven J. Wurzelbacher

FOREWORD

Occupational safety and health research and surveillance are essential for the prevention and control of injuries, illnesses and hazards that arise from the workplace.

Research and surveillance can fill gaps in knowledge about where hazards exist and what interventions are effective at preventing workplace injuries, illnesses and fatalities. Workers' compensation insurance records are a resource used for these primary prevention purposes. In addition, workers' compensation records may be used for early detection of health outcomes in populations of workers which is part of secondary prevention. They may also be used to help identify effective medical treatment which is part of tertiary prevention.

Workers' compensation insurance covers nearly all workers in the U.S. and provides those who are injured or become ill as a result of work with

---

* This is an edited, reformatted and augmented version of DHHS (NIOSH) Publication No. 2014–110, dated January 2014; released by U.S. Department of Health and Human Ser-vices, Centers for Disease Control and Prevention, National Institute for Occupational Safety and Health.

medical treatment, a portion of lost wages, and a lump sum for some permanent impairments. Nonetheless, there are limitations to conducting studies that rely on workers' compensation records since not all injuries and illnesses result in claims being filed. Furthermore, the data that are collected are not readily combined if obtained from multiple sources since requirements vary substantially among the states.

The National Institute for Occupational Safety and Health (NIOSH) joined with a number of public and private sector co-sponsors to convene two workshops on the use of workers' compensation data for occupational safety and health. Creation of this document was suggested at the second workshop as a means to describe elements of the workers' compensation insurance programs in the U.S. and the potential to utilize the records for public health purposes.

Public health agencies, the workers' compensation industry, trade associations and the state-level programs share interests in utilizing these data to protect workers from occupational injuries and illnesses. To help facilitate these goals, NIOSH has created a Center for Workers' Compensation Studies. Further information on the center may be obtained at http://www.cdc.gov /niosh/topics/ workerComp/CWCS/.

John Howard, M.D.
Director
National Institute for Occupational Safety and Health
Centers for Disease Control and Prevention

ACKNOWLEDGMENTS

We thank the participants at the Use of Workers' Compensation Data for Occupational Safety and Health Workshop that was held in Washington, DC in June 2012 for suggesting that a document like this primer be developed. Many of those participants and other stakeholders provided essential input on the scope and contents of this primer.

We also thank the internal and external reviewers for their valuable comments.

ACRONYMS AND ABBREVIATIONS

AASCIF	American Association of State Compensation Insurance Funds
ACORD	Association for Cooperative Operations Research and Development
ACS	American Community Survey
AIA	American Insurance Association
CBP	County Business Patterns
CDC	Centers for Disease Control and Prevention
CES	Current Employment Statistics
CFOI	Census of Fatal Occupational Injuries
CFR	Code of Federal Regulations
CPS	Current Population Survey
DHHS	Department of Health and Human Services
EDI	Electronic Data Interchange
FEIN	Federal Employer Identification Number
FROI	First Report of Injury
FTE	Full-time Equivalent
HIPAA	Health Insurance Portability and Accountability Act
IAIABC	International Association of Industrial Accident Boards and Commissions
ICD	International Classification of Disease
IRS	Internal Revenue Service
MSHA	Mine Safety and Health Administration
NAICS	North American Industry Classification System
NASI	National Academy of Social Insurance
NAIC	National Association of Insurance Commissioners
NCOIL	National Conference of Insurance Legislators
NCCI	National Council on Compensation Insurance
NIOSH	National Institute for Occupational Safety and Health
OES	Occupational Employment Statistics
OIICS	Occupational Injury and Illness Classification System
OSHA	Occupational Safety and Health Administration
PCIAA	Property and Casualty Insurers Association of America
PEO	Professional Employment Organizations
QCEW	Quarterly Census of Employment and Wages
SDS	Supplementary Data System
SIC	Standard Industrial Classification System

SOC	Standard Occupational Classification System
SOII	Survey of Occupational Injuries and Illnesses
TPA	Third-party Administrator
WCIO	Workers' Compensation Insurance Organizations
WCRI	Workers' Compensation Research Institute

1. INTRODUCTION

The purpose of this document is to help public health researchers and practitioners, particularly those in occupational safety and health, to broaden their understanding of workers' compensation insurance, relevant aspects of the insurance industry records, and the potential uses of that information for public health purposes. Workers' compensation insurance has been established in all states to provide income protection, medical treatment, and rehabilitation for employees who are injured or become ill as a result of work. Workers' compensation claims and medical treatment records along with other information resources have been used to conduct occupational safety and health research and surveillance and to identify intervention needs.

Several government agencies and private organizations sponsored two workshops in September 2009 and June 2012 on the use of workers' compensation data for occupational safety and health purposes. The workshops featured discussions of opportunities for collaboration in the analysis of workers' compensation data in order to help reduce the risks of occupational injuries and illnesses. Participants included representatives from private insurance carriers, insurance associations, self-insured corporations, academic institutions and government agencies.

Presentations in the first workshop described differences among state laws, proper interpretation of common industry terms, proprietary interests in insurance data, public release of internal analyses, methods for linking workers' compensation records with other health and employment records, and independent analysis of claims data by health scientists, economists and government agencies (NIOSH 2010; Utterback et al. 2012). One of the principal messages from the first workshop was that even though workers' compensation records are primarily designed and used by the insurance industry to administer claims, public health investigators are interested in them for prevention and control of occupational injuries and illnesses. The interested parties have different perspectives on the value and potential uses of workers' compensation data. Relationships would need to build trust and respect for the various stakeholder perspectives to foster collaboration.

The second workshop included discussions of six draft white papers along with 35 platform and poster presentations on research with workers' compensation data (NIOSH 2013a). Although much progress is being made in understanding the merits of workers' compensation data resources, significant limitations exist. For example, these data appear to constitute an incomplete record of occupational injuries and illnesses at the state level. While standards for collecting and compiling the data exist, they are not universally used. Some fields on the record forms are often blank or incomplete and essential information for public health purposes, such as occupation, race, ethnicity, and duration of employment, may not be recorded. Multiple parties add data to the records at various stages as claims work their ways through the employees, employers, medical facilities, third-party administrators and state agencies. Nonetheless, important public health research can be conducted with available data as long as the limitations and their effects on generalizability are considered.

At the end of the second workshop, some commented that the public health and the insurance communities may have different interpretations of terms in common usage and overcoming that barrier might be facilitated by a summary of the workers' compensation industry and a crosswalk of terminology used by each group. A team began work on this document as a result.

Following the background and brief history of the workers' compensation programs in the U.S., this primer describes: (1) benefits and premiums; (2) the relationship between premiums and safety incentives; (3) roles of insurers, state agencies and third party administrators; (4) types of policies; (5) claims and other workers' compensation insurance information on medical treatments, costs and disability status; (6) limitations of current industry data standards; (7) loss prevention programs; and (8) public health research, surveillance and regulations. A glossary of workers' compensation terms begins on page 35 and a guide for prospective research and surveillance projects follows on page 41.

2. BACKGROUND

The economic and social burden of occupational injuries and illnesses can only be roughly estimated (Leigh and Marcin 2012; Leigh 2011).

Uncertainties are due to many factors including: (1) workers receive only a portion of regular wages through workers' compensation; (2) occupational illnesses are frequently not compensated; (3) medical treatment costs for many occupational injuries are paid by other insurance; (4) insurance data are fragmented; and (5) data are protected for proprietary and personal identification purposes. No central repository for workers' compensation claims information exists in the U.S. The National Academy of Social Insurance (NASI), a non-governmental organization, produces an annual report on workers' compensation insurance. The most recent version, Workers' Compensation Benefits, Coverage, and Costs, 2010, states that workers' compensation insurance covered more than 124 million U.S. workers at a total estimated cost to employers of $71 billion in 2010 (Sengupta et al. 2012). Total insured medical payments to providers and insured cash benefits to workers were estimated at $28.1 billion and $29.5 billion, respectively.

Most workers' compensation insurance carriers are private entities except for exclusive state insurance funds in North Dakota, Ohio, Washington and Wyoming. Also, twenty states offer state-sponsored nonprofit competitive insurance companies or state licensed mutual insurance plans, some to only selected portions of the market such as those employers that are unable to obtain insurance coverage in the voluntary market. There are typically dozens if not hundreds of private carriers in each state. Large employers in the U.S. are often self-insured under rules established by the states.

Workers' Compensation Records

Workers' compensation insurance, in various forms, covers in excess of 90% of the U.S. wage and salary workers (Sengupta et al. 2012). Ideally, each workplace injury or illness requiring medical care covered by workers' compensation would result in a record being created for the claim. The primary purpose for the record is to ensure proper payment to injured or ill workers and to the medical providers. Yet the record may contain useful information for public health purposes on the nature of the injury or disorder, the partof-body, the event or exposure, industry sector, occupation, and the worker's ability to continue working or disability status. Descriptive contents may provide additional information on materials related to the event such as biological, chemical, ergonomic or physical hazards.

Medical records for workers' compensation cases can provide further information about the extent and severity of the injury plus information about the injured workers such as gender, age, race/ethnicity, and other chronic health conditions that may exacerbate an injury. Workers' compensation medical records also identify disabilities that result from the occupational injuries or illnesses and billing records can contain information on treatments and costs for the medical portion of the claims.

Insurance carriers and self-insured entities are required to provide state government agencies with claims information that is used for administrative requirements such as oversight and to conduct hearings for adjudication of disputes. The level of detail and quality of information vary among the data providers. Nonetheless, in each state, a government agency has longitudinal data that may be suitable for public health research and surveillance purposes. It is noteworthy that the Health Insurance Portability and Accountability Act (HIPAA) Privacy Rule exempts workers' compensation medical information from its disclosure restrictions.[1]

If information from multiple sources or jurisdictions could be combined, workers' compensation insurance records would permit better analysis and tracking of occupational injuries and some diseases. In public health, use of these tracking systems is called surveillance. (See box for a definition.) Health scientists, economists, and others use large surveillance data sets for informative analyses of trends in incidence and costs, identification of health hazards associated with new technologies, evaluation of injury and illness prevention program effectiveness, and to provide employers with information needed to protect their workforce.

> The U.S. Centers for Disease Control and Prevention (CDC) defines public health surveillance as the "ongoing systematic collection, analysis, and interpretation of health data essential to the planning, implementation, and evaluation of public health practices, closely integrated with the timely dissemination of these data to those who need to know."

Limitations on Records Utility

For public health research and surveillance purposes, workers' compensation data are likely to be more representative of population risks for acute injuries than they are for occupational illnesses. Some investigators have used limited workers' compensation data to estimate the frequency, magnitude, severity, and cost of compensated injuries and to examine trends over time. Several papers at the 2012 workshop described deficiencies in workers' compensation records for injury and illness surveillance purposes, even for more severe injuries such as amputations, fractures and concussions (NIOSH 2013a).

Combining workers' compensation data from a number of jurisdictions is a major technical challenge. Each state legislature and the District of Columbia establish workers' compensation requirements[2] with significant variations. For example, states vary in the coverage of compensable cumulative injuries such as carpal tunnel syndrome, levels of payments for partial and total disability, both temporary and permanent, and the minimum number of days away from work to qualify for wage-replacement compensation. In many states, employers with small numbers of employees, temporary employees and other groups, such as farm employees, are excluded from coverage requirements. Certain groups of workers such as railroad, longshore, many maritime and all Federal employees are covered by rules established at the national level. Special compensation funds have been established at the Federal level for atomic weapons workers and for those disabled by black lung disease.

Another factor that makes it difficult to combine data from multiple sources is the lack of national data standards. For example, although some nationally standardized data coding systems are available, such as Occupational Injury and Illnesses Classification System (OIICS), and North American Industry Classification System (NAICS), they are not universally used across the states. In fact, workers' compensation rate-making bodies like the National Council on Compensation Insurance (NCCI) and several state rating bureaus use coding systems that pre-date OIICS and NAICS systems. These coding systems are discussed in subsequent chapters.

Furthermore, access to workers' compensation data can be difficult to obtain. Insurance carriers are usually private businesses that manage very large data sets in integrated, proprietary systems. These data are generally not shared with external groups. Some insurance organizations like NCCI routinely collect standardized data from insurance carriers in many states but their contracts protect the proprietary interests of the contributing carriers and restrict data uses to issues directly related to estimating or recommending insurance premium rates for establishments within industries. Only one private insurance entity, The Liberty Mutual Research Institute for Safety, has published extensive peer-review articles related to injury and illness prevention based on workers' compensation records (Courtney 2010).

Even when conducting analyses of workers' compensation data from a single state, there are characteristics of the workers' compensation data that limit its utility. Multiple researchers have reported limitations on the utilization of workers' compensation for occupational injury and illness research and surveillance. Azaroff, et al. (2002) described a number of filters that limit the reporting and filing of cases and the subsequent development of a medical record or workers' compensation claim following a workplace injury or illness. Several investigators have reported much less than full participation in workers' compensation for occupational injuries and illnesses with up to half or more of the compensable claims going unreported (Biddle et al. 1998; Rosenman et al. 2000; Fan et al. 2006; Scherzer et al. 2008; Lipscomb et al. 2009). Leigh (2012) estimated that only 21% of the total economic burden of occupational injuries and illnesses was paid by workers' compensation insurance carriers. Others describe the difficulty in estimating the portion of the burden that is shifted to other social and health insurance programs (Boden et al. 2001) such as when workers with occupational injuries and illnesses file disability claims with the Social Security Administration (O'Leary et al. 2012).

3. Brief History of Workers' Compensation in the US

Following European examples from the 19th century, states in the U.S. began to develop workers' compensation laws in the early 1900's to address the increasing risks of occupational injuries and illnesses associated with the industrial revolution. Initial laws in several states were declared unconstitutional but, in 1911, Wisconsin became the first state to establish a workers' compensation system that withstood constitutional challenges in the courts. By 1920, most states and territories[3] had followed suit. Mississippi was the last state to adopt a workers' compensation law in 1948.[4] These laws provide partial benefits to affected workers and protect employers from tort suits for occupational injuries and illnesses in nearly all cases. This "grand bargain" circumvents lengthy, expensive trials where the burden of proof was on the employee and removed a source of financial uncertainty for the employer.

Since the beginning of workers' compensation programs in the U.S., nearly all employers have been required to have insurance to cover payments for: (1) medical costs resulting from occupational injuries and some occupational illnesses suffered by workers; and (2) partial replacement of injured or ill workers' lost wages, also known as indemnity. Death benefits are paid to survivors for occupational fatalities. These benefits are paid only for claims where workers were injured or became ill due to conditions that "arise out of and in the course of employment," with restrictions that vary substantially among the 50 states due to legislation and case law. In return for this coverage, employers are granted immunity from employee law suits (tort litigation) for nearly all occupational injuries and illnesses. Thus workers' compensation insurance is structured to be the sole employee remedy for restitution subsequent to occupational injuries and illnesses. Some exceptions exist for willful injuries and gross negligence.

Mandatory Coverage

Each state has its own set of requirements about which employers are compelled to obtain workers' compensation insurance. Varying factors are generally the industry sector of the employer, the minimum number of employees, length of employment, and, in some cases, the familial relationship of the employee with the employer. The minimum number of employees requiring provision of workers' compensation coverage varies between one and five across the states. Some states exclude agricultural employers with less than a specified number of employees. Some states exclude self-employed workers while other states provide an option for their coverage. Some states exclude corporate officers in limited liability corporations without other employees. Other states have specific workers' compensation rules for industry sectors such as mining and construction. The employment relationships of employers with employees versus contractors are clearly defined in many states.[5]

Since the enactment of Texas workers' compensation legislation in 1913, employers in that state have been allowed to voluntarily participate in workers' compensation insurance coverage. Those employers who choose to opt out of coverage are not protected from tort suits by the injured or ill workers, or by surviving family members in case of fatalities. Any medical expenses are the responsibility of the injured or ill workers. No payments are required for the workers' lost earnings for the duration of their recovery period or for permanent disabilities. More recently, Oklahoma legislation that was enacted in May 2013 allows employers to opt out of workers' compensation insurance. In this state, employers who opt out are required to have an internal compensation program for occupational injuries and illnesses that is consistent with Employee Retirement Income Security Act (ERISA) (Oklahoma Insurance Department 2013).

Basis for Insurance Premiums

Throughout the history of workers' compensation in the U.S., premiums for insurance policies have been determined by a set of factors related to employer risks, primarily the mix of occupational classes they employ. Employers are assigned to work classifications[6] according to state-sanctioned rating bureau guidelines. In general, employers in classifications with greater injury and illness risks and loss costs have higher "manual rates." For example, a roofing contractor generally has a higher manual rate than a bank. Recommended or specified manual rates must be approved by the state regulators in most cases. Additionally, those employers which qualify for experience rating and that have a history of greater injury and illness claims and costs within the risk classes are charged even higher premiums through the application of an experience modification factor. Those employers with fewer claims and lower loss costs benefit from lower premiums.

Motivations for Prevention

From the beginning of workers' compensation insurance laws in the U.S., the experience modification factor was intended to encourage employers to invest in safety. A history of elevated claims frequencies and costs results in higher insurance premiums for the employer. Adoption of effective safety strategies reduces occupational injuries and illnesses which should decrease future premiums. Additionally, many states have enacted legislation that requires carriers to provide premium discounts for the presence of employer-based leading indicators such as safety and health programs which meet specific criteria. Moreover, most carriers provide loss prevention services to client employers in order to limit escalation of claims costs and insurance premiums. Some states, for example Texas, Missouri and Arkansas, mandate that insurance carriers provide loss prevention services to clients and many specify that the services shall be provided at no additional cost beyond the annual premium.

Recent Changes in the Industry and Market

The workers' compensation insurance market is dynamic. Both the nature of work and workforce are changing. In recent years, the mix of industries and technologies in the U.S. have changed and the workforce is aging (Restrepo and Shuford 2011) and increasingly non-English speaking (Hakimzadeh and Cohn 2007) and obese (Ostbye et al. 2007; Trogden et al. 2007; Schmid et al. 2012). In the past couple of decades, there have been substantial changes in state laws that affect workers' compensation policies and procedures. Workers' compensation insurance requirements on issues such as managed care organizations, limited physician choice, vocational rehabilitation, minimum standards of care, and restrictions on treatment options have been enacted in many states. Meanwhile, medical costs for claims have escalated (Shuford et al. 2009) and litigation of claims is common in many states (Willborn et al. 2012).

Changes in the relationships between employees and employers have created needs for newer workers' compensation insurance policy types. For example, contingent work arrangements through temporary employment agencies and professional employer organizations (PEO) are becoming more common (Smith et al. 2010). These emergent work arrangements can complicate coverage and incentives for injury prevention. PEOs primarily have provided human resource and management services to client employers although they increasingly employ workers in other industries. PEOs result in co-employment by the host agency and the client employer. Newer workers' compensation policy arrangements have been developed for PEOs and similar employment leasing organizations (Shuford 2013) since a single host agency may employ workers at different times in industries with various risk classifications.

In contrast, workers who are employees of a temporary agency are covered under the workers' compensation policy for that agency, not that of the client employer. Independent contractors, which are defined in the workers' compensation statutes in many states, are not covered by the policy of the contracting employer, e.g. the general contractor at a construction site. Also, independent contractors which are self-employed persons are qualified for workers' compensation insurance in some, but not all, states. Each of these arrangements can blur the responsibility for provision of workers' compensation coverage and has resulted in a lack of coverage for some workers.

Insurance Industry Resources

Many organizations produce information that is used by various parts of the workers' compensation insurance industry. The U.S. Department of Labor formerly compiled reports on benefits and costs and annual summaries of changes in state workers' compensation requirements. They also employed regional experts on workers' compensation. The federal efforts have shifted and some of the products have been replaced by private or nonprofit entities such as NASI and a number of others. For example, a biannual report that compares the average cost of workers' compensation insurance per $100 of employer payroll among states is published by the State of Oregon (Oregon Department of Consumer and Business Services 2012). The roles and contributions of a number of these insurance organizations appears later in this document.

Effectiveness of State Laws

The comparative impact of the various state requirements has been a source of debate over the entire history of workers' compensation in the U.S. Federalization of the programs has been suggested from time to time. The Occupational Safety and Health Act in 1970 created the National Commission on State Workers' Compensation Laws which, after public meetings and comment period, proposed Federal minimum standards for state programs if the states did not substantially improve their laws. Related Congressional actions failed to pass. The Commission did develop a set of recommendations for the state programs.[7] Changes in state requirements subsequent to those recommendations have been periodically reviewed which indicate partial adoption by each of the states.[8]

According to national surveillance data, the frequency and rate of occupational injuries have declined over the past several decades (Sengupta et al. 2012; U.S. Bureau of Labor Statistics 2012). In 2010, employer costs for workers' compensation benefits as a proportion of payroll were at the lowest level in 30 years (Sengupta et al. 2012). There has also been a general trend across the states to limit compensation for disabled workers (Spieler and Burton 2012). Whether the surveillance trends are due to reduced injuries, increases in underreporting, or other factors is the subject of ongoing research.

4. WORKERS' COMPENSATION INSURANCE BENEFITS

Payments for workers' compensation claims can be for employee medical treatment, loss of wages (indemnity), vocational rehabilitation, permanent disability, and death. The rules for the level of payment vary tremendously among the states with a few exceptions. First, all medical expenses are the responsibility of the insurance provider without co-payment by the claimant but may be subject to legislated time limits and to medical fee schedules. These covered costs include the initial treatment and subsequent treatments plus physical therapy or vocational rehabilitations. Second, indemnity payments to the worker who misses work for greater than the minimum waiting period are provided tax-free. Third, most states provide wage replacement payments for the initial waiting period after lost work time exceeds a number of days that is set by the individual states (Table 1). For example, if the initial waiting period for indemnity payments is five calendar days, payments for that initial period would be made once the lost work time on that claim exceeds a separate minimum period such as 21 calendar days. This latter minimum time period is called the retroactive period.

Table 1. Waiting period for claimant to receive wage replacement benefits and the retroactive period which, if exceeded, results in payment for the waiting period

State	Waiting Period (days)[1]	Retroactive (days)[2]
AL	3	21
AK	3	28
AR	7	14
AZ	7	14
CA	3	14
CO	3	14
CT	3	14
DE	3	7
DC	3	14
FL	7	21
GA	7	21
HI	3	
ID	5	14
IL	3	14
IN	7	21
IA	3	14

State	Waiting Period (days)[1]	Retroactive (days)[2]
KS	7	21
KY	7	14
LA	7	42
ME	7	14
MD	3	14
MA	5	21
MI	7	14
MN	3	10
MS	5	14
MO	3	14
MT	4	
NE	7	42
NV	5	6
NH	3	14
NJ	7	7
NM	7	28
NY	7	14
NC	7	21
ND	5	5
OH	7	14
OK	3	
OR	3	14
PA	7	14
RI	3	
SC	7	14
SD	7	7
TN	7	14
TX	7	14
UT	3	14
VT	3	10
VA	7	21
WA	3	14
WV	3	7
WI	3	7
WY	3	9

[1] The minimum number of days away from work to qualify for indemnity payments, also known as the waiting period.

[2] If away from work for a number of days in excess of the retroactive period, claimant qualifies for indemnity payment for the waiting period.

Source: 2011 Chambers of Commerce Workers' Compensation Laws, Chart IX, (see caveats pp. 78 – 79 in reference)

Temporary Disabilities

Temporary and permanent disability benefits can be in the form of partial or total benefits. Temporary partial benefits would be merited when workers are away from work beyond the specified minimum period but able to return to work in a limited capacity that would partially affect their income. Temporary total disability benefits occur when the worker is unable to be employed in any capacity for a period of time that exceeds the specified waiting period. Many states have set time limits on temporary total disability indemnity payments such as 104 weeks. These benefits may convert to temporary partial benefits if the worker is able to return to work part-time for limited periods or if able to complete work in another position at a lower pay rate.

Permanent Disabilities

Permanent partial disability payments are awarded for workers who may no longer return to work with sufficient capacity to perform their prior duties or if they lose part or all of the function of a specific body part due to a work-related amputation or other disability. The loss of a body part or function is often compensated based on a fee schedule such that a set multiplier of the average wage is paid either as a lump sum or over a period of time. Many states also provide permanent partial coverage for disfigurement of the face or other body parts.

The extent of permanent partial disability is determined by the degree of impairment at the point of "maximal medical improvement" in order to settle the case. Impairment is usually determined according to medical references such as the American Medical Association Guides to the Evaluation of Permanent Impairment (Cocchiarella and Anderson 2001).

Permanent total disability indemnity payments are made to those workers who can no longer be employed in any capacity. Depending on the state, these payments may continue until retirement age, for the life of the individual, or until disability payments are received from another source such as the Social Security Administration.

In some cases, the portions of the disability that are attributed to work and non-work conditions can factor in the amount of the disability payment. For example, in some jurisdictions, a worker who is disabled as a result of occupational exposures to a respiratory hazard may have their benefits reduced if a non-occupational exposure, such as smoking, is demonstrated to have contributed to the impairment.

Death benefits are paid to survivors of the worker who was killed on the job. The level ofbenefits usually varies with the number of dependents. Although generally a function of the average weekly wage, death benefits are often limited by a minimum and maximum amount but may last for the lifetime of the surviving spouse or until dependent children attain 18 years of age or older in certain cases.

Settlement of Claims

Lump sum settlements, also known as negotiated settlements or compromise and release agreements, in lieu of limited periodic payments, have been increasing for disabilities covered by workers' compensation insurance. These agreements are reached between the disabled employee, the employer and the insurance provider. In some states, settlements may cover only indemnity portions of a claim, with future medical benefits provided, while others allow payouts for future medical care (including Medicare set-asides,[9] if appropriate). Often times, the settlements must be approved by a state workers' compensation authority.

Claim Costs and Reserves

Claims that are not settled through mutual agreement remain open until all payments for medical treatments, rehabilitation and indemnity have been completed and the worker returns to work, reaches the maximum indemnity period or retirement age or dies. As a result, the cost of a claim can continue to grow. Future obligations on a claim are handled in the form of reserves that are established for open ended claims and are dependent on the nature of the injury and the likelihood of the rehabilitation of the worker. Reserves typically represent estimates of the most likely future cost of the claim, which approximates the mode of the distribution of claims of that type, rather than the mean.

With the open-ended nature of longer duration claims, insurance carriers often value (estimate cost of) the claims based on the payments made to date, the payments plus reserves, or the payments plus reserves as of a certain period of time, such as 30 months after the date of injury. Claims can also be valued using "factor-adjusted" methods that calculate costs by applying actuarial loss development factors that attempt to estimate the ultimate payout amounts for the claims. For the "factor-adjusted" method, reserves therefore represent the mean future cost of claims of the same type. This method is applied to groups of claims and is used by insurance underwriters for analyzing aggregated claims for loss trends. A potential drawback with "factor-adjusted" methods is that their values are usually higher than the actual values of the individual claim (since the mean is always higher than the mode and median in claim cost distributions) (Wurzelbacher et al. 2013). Some carriers use yet other cost valuation methods.

5. Workers' Compensation Insurance Providers

The workers' compensation insurance industry is complex with total per annum expenditures in excess of $70 billion (Sengupta et al. 2012). The primary types of groups in the industry include insurance carriers, state regulatory agencies, third-party administrators and numerous trade organizations. Insurance providers may be privately-held corporations, mutual corporations (owned by the policy holders), and state or Federal agencies. All states except North Dakota permit self-insurance for qualified employers (U.S. Chamber of Commerce 2012).

Insurance Providers and Policies

The insurance providers are regulated by individual state requirements. Even nationwide insurance carriers must follow the requirements in each of the states where they offer coverage. In most states, private insurance carriers compete in the regulated voluntary market. Twenty states offer alternatives to the private insurers in the form of non-profit state-sponsored insurance programs. In addition, state funds are the exclusive providers of workers' compensation insurance in four states – North Dakota, Ohio, Washington and Wyoming.

Insurance providers employ a range of specialists such as actuaries, adjusters, underwriters, claims administrators and loss control consultants (see glossary). Brokers directly market insurance policies to employers and they may offer policies from a single insurance carrier or multiple competing carriers. Many private insurance providers specialize in specific industry sectors in which they are most familiar with risks. Large national carriers offer insurance across diverse sectors but may still focus on certain industries. Many private insurance providers also offer other lines of coverage beyond workers' compensation, such as property and liability.

Insurance providers typically issue annual policies. An employer may opt to change insurance carrier on the anniversary of the policy except in states with exclusive funds. Annual policies add to the competitiveness of the market yet they reduce the investment commitment of a carrier to client employers. For example, carriers are not likely to invest in cost reduction strategies such as safety equipment if the recovery of the investment would take several years to materialize.

Residual Market

The residual market customarily consists of those employers that are unable to obtain insurance coverage in the voluntary market. The residual market usually serves newer employers without sufficient years of experience in workers' compensation, employers with poor claims experience or employers in high-risk industries unable to obtain a policy to underwrite their potential losses. However, the residual market in some states may include employers that voluntarily participate when there are economic or services advantages. All 24 state-sponsored insurance programs provide coverage for their residual markets. A few of the state-sponsored government insurance programs provide insurance coverage only to the residual market. Some states require the private insurance companies in their markets to write proportionate coverage for the residual market employers in the form of assigned-risk pools. The Burton primer on workers' compensation provides additional details on the residual market and assigned-risk pools (Burton 2004).

6. State Workers' Compensation Agencies

Each state has an agency that provides administrative services for workers' compensation, has adjudicatory responsibilities in cases of disputes, and/or develops regulations and rules for the workers' compensation system consistent with the intent of legislative mandates. Portions of the agencies may operate as commissions, bureaus, or departments. They may be affiliated with other levels of government in the states such as labor, industry, insurance or commerce.

Collection of Records

All states require that some portion of the workers' compensation claims records be reported to the agency by employers (Table 2). In some cases only indemnity claims are reported yet in others all claims (including medical only claims) are reported. More and more states have developed automatic Web (internet)-based or telemetric reporting systems that use standard forms and require the use of standardized codes for fields in the forms. For example, the Workers' Compensation Insurance Organization (WCIO) part-of-body, nature of injury or illness, and cause of incident codes are used in nearly all jurisdictions.

State agencies may be restricted by requirements in the portions of the workers' compensation records which may be released to the public. In some states, those restrictions can extend to other in-state agencies as well. It bears repeating that HIPAA Privacy Rule exempts workers' compensation medical information from its disclosure restrictions.

Other Roles of State Agencies

Many state agencies oversee special funds that provide benefits to injured or ill workers whose employer failed to obtain the legally required coverage. Most states also offer second injury funds which reimburse employers for certain claims paid to workers with pre-existing injuries. A few state agencies, e.g. Ohio and Washington, provide safety grants to offset some portion of an employer's expenses for installation of safety equipment. Grants in other states, e.g. Massachusetts and Oregon, are made to support development of injury prevention training programs (Table 3).

A few states have research components in their workers' compensation agencies. These components may track expenditures, evaluate the implications of proposed legal changes, or consider other aspects of policy options. Many states, e.g. Florida (Florida Division of Workers' Compensation 2011), develop annual reports for their agencies that reveal the number of cases in various categories such as indemnity, medical-only and disallowed claims as well as the number of claims that are contested by the employer or the insurance provider. The reports may also describe recent changes to the requirements and the status of claims that are open and those that are closed. Other data may be presented on the average cost of claims for various injury and illness types as well as the distribution of claims across industry segments.

Web (Internet) Services

Most state agencies provide diverse services and extensive information via Web sites. Available services include injury, illness and death claim forms for employees and employers and the means to report suspected fraud. Proof of insurance coverage by individual employers may be obtained in some states through their Web sites. The Web site information may describe the rights and responsibilities of employees, employers, insurance carriers, medical providers, and the state agency according to requirements in the state. Many states provide plain-language guides for employees and employers that explain claims processing and appeals. Ombudsmen in some states may be contacted through the Web sites to assist claimants.

Most state agencies also use Web sites to promote safe and healthful working conditions and to provide information on safety and health program aids that can be readily used by employers. Other information on participation in various programs associated with premium discounts or penalties is offered as well. Lists of insurance providers as well as consultants and third party administrators are available on many state sites. Training on the workers' compensation requirements is often made available through the Web sites. Links to state statutes and regulations are common.

7. Third-Party Administrators

Third-party administrators (TPA) are insurance organizations other than the brokers, providers, associations and the state agencies. TPAs provide a wide range of services. They often complete the actual claims forms and may be the direct payer of benefits to workers and to medical providers. They can be the intermediary that reports the claim information to the respective state agency and they provide analytical reports to their clients. Self-insured businesses often employ TPAs for a diverse range of claim and insurance services. TPAs may complete and otherwise process claim forms for the employer, pool or group including an initial determination of compensability. Complete risk management information systems are offered by some TPAs.

In addition, they can provide services such as medical case management, medical bill review, and programs for the injured employee to returnto-work. Some TPAs provide investigation, subrogation and legal services to their clients. Pharmacy benefit management and Medicare set-aside services are some of the later additions to the TPA offerings. Yet others may provide loss prevention services and health and safety training for employees and employers. TPAs may also provide clients with their required Occupational Safety and Health Administration (OSHA) logs for recordable injuries and illnesses.

8. Types of Policies

Workers' compensation insurance policies vary in many ways. The most straightforward policies cover the claims costs due to a worker injury or illness experienced by a single employer at a single business establishment, i.e. location. Some employers have multiple establishments for a single policy and the risk classification for the individual establishments may be different, e.g. a manufacturer that also has a retail outlet. Yet other policies may cover workers at multiple establishments that change over time such as one for a company in the residential construction industry.

Table 2. Required employer reporting of injuries, illnesses and deaths to State Workers' Compensation Bureaus

State	Medical Treatment beyond 1st Aid Provided[1]	Indemnity Only (Min. No.Days)[2,3]
AL		Y(3)
AK	Y	
AR	Y	
AZ	Y	
CA		Y(1)
CO		Y(3)
CT		Y(1)
DE	Y	
DC	Y	
FL	Y	
GA		Y(7)

State	Medical Treatment beyond 1st Aid Provided[1]	Indemnity Only (Min. No.Days)[2,3]
HI	Y	
ID	Y	Y(1)[4]
IL		Y(3)
IN		Y(1)
IA		Y(3)
KS		Y(1)
KY		Y(1)
LA		Y(7)
ME		Y(1)
MD		Y(3)
MA		Y(5)
MI		Y(7)
MN		Y(3)
MS		Y(5)
MO	Y	
MT	Y	
NE	Y	
NV	Y	
NH	Y	
NJ	Y	
NM	Y	
NY		Y(1)
NC		Y(1)
ND	Y	
OH		Y(7)
OK	Y	
OR		Y(3)
PA		Y(1)
RI	Y	Y(3) [4]
SC	>$500	Y(1) [4]
SD	Y	Y(7) [4]
TN	Y	
TX		Y(1)
UT	Y	
VT	Y	Y(1) [4]
VA		Y
WA		Y(1)

Table 2. (Continued)

State	Medical Treatment beyond 1st Aid Provided[1]	Indemnity Only (Min. No.Days)[2,3]
WV	Y	
WI		Y(3)
WY	Y	

[1]If Y, employers are required to report all claims that result in medical treatment beyond first aid to the workers' compensation bureau. (In SC, all claims with >$500 in medical expenses must be reported.)

[2]Employers are required to report all claims for occupational injuries and illnesses for workers missing work for a period of time in excess of these values.

[3]All deaths due to occupational injuries or illnesses must also be reported in all states.

[4]Additional reporting required for disabilities in excess of the number of days indicated.

Source: 2011 Chambers of Commerce Workers' Compensation Laws, Chart IX, (see caveats pp. 78 – 79 in reference)

Table 3. States with statutes, rules and/or regulations about employer-based occupational safety and health program elements plus states with approved state OSHA Plans or consultation programs only, 2011

State OS&H Regulations	States
Requirements	
Employer Written Safety and Health Program	CA[1], HI[2], LA[3], MN[4], NE, NV[5], NH[5], NC[6],WA
Employer/Employee Safety and Health Committee	AL[7], CA[4], CT[8], MN[9], MT[10], NE, NV[11], NH[10], NC[12], OR[13], TN[14], WA[5]
Insurer to Provide Loss Prevention Services	AR, CA, KS, MS, MO, MT, NM, OR, PA, RI, SD, TX
On-Site Inspection by Loss Prevention Services	AR[15], CA[16], DE[17], NM[18], NY[19], RI[20], TX[21]
Incentives	
Premium Reduction for Safety Program Elements	CO, DE[22], FL, HI, ME, NH, NM, NY, ND, OH, OK, PA, SD[23], UT[24], WI, WY[25]
Employer Penalty for Violation of Rule at Time of Injury	CA, IL, MA, MO, NC, WI
Safety Grant	MA[26], MN, NY, ND, OH, OR[26],UT, WA
Registry of S&H Practitioners	HI, LA, MO

State OS&H Regulations	States
State OSHA Plan	AK, AZ, CA, CT[27], HI, IL[27], IN, IA, KY, MD, MI, MN, NV, NJ[27], NM, NY[27], NC, OR, SC, TN, UT, VT, VA, WA, WY
State Consultation Program Only	AL, AR, CO, DE, FL, GA, ID, KS, LA, ME, MA, MS, MO, MT, NE, NH, ND, OH, OK, PA, RI, SD, TX, WV, WI

Information in this table was obtained from Web sites of state legislatures and agencies. Due to the difficulty in locating statutes, rules, regulations and relevant case law, some information may have been omitted from the table. Further information may be obtained from the primary author.

[1]Reduced documentation requirements if <10 employees; <20 employees and not on high hazard list and experience modification is <1.1; or < 20 employees and on designated low-hazard list.

[2]If >24 employees

[3]If > 15 employees

[4]For high hazard industries on list

[5]If >10 employees

[6]If experience modification factor is >1.5

[7]Upon written request of an employee

[8]If >25 employees or injury and illness rate greater than average for industry

[9]If > 25 employees or if in top 10% within industry lost-days rate or if top 25% of pure premium for all classes

[10]If >5 employees

[11]If >25 employees

[12]If >10 employees and experience modification factor >1.5

[13]Routine safety meetings also allowed

[14]If experience modification factor is >1.2

[15]Or other appropriate services if premium > $25,000, or if > $5,000 and loss ratio > 100%, or if loss ratio > 150%

[16]For targeted high hazard employers

[17]Fee is charged and employer required to participate in Workplace Safety Program discount

[18]If premium > $5,000, self-inspection is allowed

[19]If payroll > $800,000 and experience modification factor >1.2

[20]If premium > $25,000 and requested by employer

[21]If premium > $25,000 and loss ratio >1.0, or if premium > $5,000 and loss ratio > 2.5

[22]If premium > $3,161

[23]Unspecified penalty for establishments where deficiency has not been corrected at time of subsequent safety review

[24]If experience modification factor >1.0 or if 3-year loss ratio > 100% and if "work place safety program" not adopted after request from the insurer then 5% premium surcharge is allowed

[25]Based on reduced loss ratio attainment

[26]Grants available for training only

[27]Public sector employees only are covered by the state plan along with consultation program for most private businesses

If employees of the business routinely travel to other states, provisions that cover losses in the other states may be added to policies. If the business has employees located in multiple states, multiple policies are typically required. With workers' compensation records alone, it may be difficult to associate an injury or illness with an establishment when the policy covers multiple establishments.

In many states, employers are allowed to form groups or pools to obtain insurance in the voluntary markets or to combine as a self-insured entity. Membership in a group is usually restricted to similar industries. Other insurance arrangements include carve-outs, which are labor/management agreements,[10] and captives, i.e. an insurance company that is wholly-owned by a single employer or a group of employers and provides insurance to the owners' businesses.

Risk Retention

Workers' compensation insurance policies determine the amount of risk the employer retains for workplace injuries and illnesses. Risk retention may increase employer interest in reducing potential losses through safety and health prevention since they could be responsible for payments on some claims. In order of increasing risk retention by the employer are the following insurance or policy types: guaranteed cost, dividend, retrospective rating, deductible, and self-insurance (Thamann and Reitz 2000). For example, with a guaranteed cost policy, the loss to the employer in a given policy year can never be more than the policy premium. On the other hand, with large deductible policies, the employer is self-insured up to an amount of the deductible yet obtains an insurance policy for excess coverage purchased from a provider. The deductible amounts may be per claim and/or aggregate and range from a few thousands of dollars to $1 million or more. Nonetheless, the carrier of the excess coverage is, according to the state regulators, responsible for the entire claim amount. The carrier then obtains reimbursement from the client employer through an agreed mechanism.

Self-insurance is a form of insurance that is generally limited to larger employers which demonstrate to their state workers' compensation regulating agency that they have the financial resources to make the equivalent of indemnity, medical and death benefit payments to their employees who suffer occupational injuries and illnesses. Qualifications for self-insurance vary among the states. For example, some require surety bonds. In Ohio, an exclusive state program, self-insurance is permitted only for those employers with a minimum of 500 employees.

Other Policies

As mentioned earlier, state-sponsored programs also provide insurance coverage for workers whose employer failed to obtain the required insurance policy. Most states also provide special coverage for second injuries which reduces the financial disincentives of employing a worker with an existing disability.

9. Policy Premiums

Premiums for workers' compensation insurance policies are determined by the risk classification of the insured employer, the size of the payroll, and in many cases, on the employer's past claims experience. "Manual rates" or "base rates" are set for each of the industry risk classes by actuarial organizations like NCCI and are expressed as the cost of insurance per $100 in payroll. The manual rate is then adjusted using an experience modification factor for those employers who are sufficiently large to be rated based on their claims history. The premium setting process and related terms are more fully explained in other sources such as A Primer on Workers' Compensation by John F. Burton, Jr.[11]

Experience Modification Factor

In general, an employer's history of increasing numbers of claims and costs leads to higher experience ratings and higher overall premiums. The experience modification factor is usually affected more by the frequency of claims from the policy holder than by the total cost, although these rules vary among the states. The loss ratio is one of the factors used to calculate premiums and it is equal to the total costs for losses divided by total premiums paid. The loss ratio may be calculated for a single client, a risk class or for the insurance industry as a whole.

Other Premium Adjustments

The premium may be further altered by discounts that are awarded for multiple reasons. For example, discounts may encourage certain activities such as an employer's participation in a safety council, having joint labor management health and safety committees, or having documented safety and health programs. Some provide premium discounts for firms with drug and alcohol programs. Many mutual insurance companies provide dividends that effectively reduce the premiums.

10. Workers' Compensation Records

Workers' compensation claims records contain information that may be used to determine the frequency of injuries and illnesses plus indicators of morbidity severity such as medical treatments, their costs, hospitalizations, days away from work, types and percentages of disabilities, and rehabilitation. As mandated by the individual state laws, parts of workers' compensation records and record systems may be completed by employees, employers, medical providers, insurance carriers, third-party administrators, and the state agencies.

The most common types of records are the claims forms for injury and illness and these are required in all states.

Yet other potentially useful records may be collected and retained by the carrier. These additional records may describe employer safety and health programs, work-site inspections and other loss prevention activities. Records may also exist on the current insurance status of individual employers, carrier enrollments to conduct business in the state, registrations of consultants and third-party administrators, adjudications and appeals, and self-insurance applications, among others. Access to these records may be restricted by the applicable laws in each state. Individual investigators need to verify all legal restrictions in each state of interest.

Standard Records

The most common claims record is the first report of injury (FROI) form. The form collects some demographic information on the injured or ill employee, disability status, and contact information for the employer, insurance carrier, and medical provider. Many states use the standard FROI developed through the Electronic Data Interchange (EDI) by the International Association of Industrial Accident Boards and Commissions (IAIABC). An example of the EDI form and instructions can be accessed at the Missouri Department of Labor and Industrial Relations Web site.[12] Three versions of this form are now in use across the participating states. Forms used by yet other states contain similar information but the range of forms is too broad to list each one of them.

The EDI forms include sections on employee wage, gender, date of birth and date of hire, occupation, employment status, and number of dependents. The event fields include date, time of day, date employer was notified and date disability began, type of injury and affected body part, and descriptive information on the equipment involved, worker activities, work process, sequence of events, and check boxes for use of personal protective equipment. Dates for return to work or for deaths are also listed on the form. The medical treatment provider is also identified and their address is listed along with a checklist for the level of treatment (from none to hospitalization), and future lost work time anticipated. Many of the fields on the FROI use standard codes which are described below in section 11.

Subsequent reports of injury (SROI) for each claim may be completed at the time treatment is provided by a health care practitioner, when a benefit type is changed (e.g. from temporary total to permanent total disability), or when the claimant returns to work or dies. Thus, a series of reports may be available for each claim. A computerized record is generally used to combine the information from the claims record series.

Billing forms from treatment providers are another set of records that provide important information. These forms list the treatment costs and may include information on diagnosis and treatments (such as Current Procedural Terminology codes) which may differ from the FROI and SROI. The differences may result from additional medical testing or from aggravation of an existing condition such as an infection. Any changes in diagnosis should be recorded in the injury claim record system.

Another record system widely used in the U.S. is the Unit Statistical Report that is provided by insurers to NCCI and other workers compensation data collection organizations. These reports are initially valued at 18 months after policy effective dates and include premium and loss information on a state basis. Open claims are valued and reported annually for up to 10 years to track loss development.[13, 14]

Limitations of Record Information

It is important to mention, once again, that the primary purpose for the injury and billing records is the timely payment of the injured or ill workers and their medical providers. Therefore, information in these records that is used for these purposes is likely to be more robust than other fields in the record systems. For example, diagnostic and treatment codes are more likely to be accurate and complete than information on occupation and employment status, particularly for medical only claims. An estimated 80% of all claims are medical only (Sengupta et al. 2012). The statutory days away from work time limits for "medical only" versus "lost time" claims vary significantly from one state to another (Table 2).

The information in many claim records evolves over time and delays in availability are to be expected. Statutes of limitation are common for workers filing claims for an occupational injury or illness and often extend to 2 years in many states. Employers are required to report claims information to state agencies within specified periods that vary among states – usually less than 15 days (Table 2). Employers and insurers are also required to maintain claims records for time periods that vary among the states. Records maintenance is one of the primary services provided to employers by TPAs.

Many of the terms used in the workers' compensation industry have specific meanings. For example, the term "claim," itself is subject to confusion as it is applied to the notification of the supervisor, notification of the insurer at the time of injury, the "first report" for the state workers' compensation agency, or a request for arbitration on the part of the worker. Some of these terms are defined in the glossary (p. 35). For any set of electronic data, it is important to obtain the applicable data dictionary that specifically defines each data element and each code used. An historical dictionary may be essential for longitudinal data. Additional limitations on claims information are described in the Background section of this document.

Disallowed and Zero-Cost Claims

Claims can be disallowed by insurance carriers or contested by the employer. The basis for denial is usually related to the degree of disability or the requirement that the injury or illness "arise out of and in the course of employment." Disallowed claims may be appealed to administrative or judicial bodies depending on the state and may result in litigation which follows established procedures in each jurisdiction.

Zero-cost claims may also occur but these are not the same as disallowed claims. The claim may have been initiated yet the injury or illness did not result in medical treatment or in lost work time. At least one state, Ohio, allows employers to pay the initial treatment and/or indemnity cost up to specified limits. If the claim is paid by the employer and remains within those limits, the claims records would indicate zero costs to the agency.

11. Standardized Codes and Systems in Workers' Compensation

Numerous standardized data coding systems are utilized for workers' compensation claims information. Some of these were specifically developed and adopted within the workers' compensation industry while other coding systems such as NAICS and International Classification of Disease (ICD) were developed for other purposes.

Standard Systems

There have been and are many attempts to standardize data for workers' compensation records. For example, WCIO led a collaborative effort to standardize codes for the part-of-body, nature of injury, and cause of event that are used across the workers' compensation insurance industry including NCCI, IAIABC and the Association for Cooperative Operations Research and Development (ACORD) but not in all jurisdictions. NCCI coding systems for industry risk classifications and a number of other factors are used in about 40 jurisdictions. IAIABC in collaboration with a number of states developed standardized forms that utilize several different data coding structures. The standards and codes have changed over time and different release versions have been adopted by states.[15] U.S. government coding systems are used extensively such as OIICS from the Bureau of Labor Statistics (BLS) and Federal Employer Identification Number (FEIN) from the Internal Revenue Service (IRS). The Standard Occupational Classification (SOC) and Standard Industry Classification (SIC) also continue to be used in some states.

Several states, e.g. California and New York, have developed their own codes for certain classes of workers' compensation information. Crosswalks may be available for some of the coding systems. Unfortunately, the comparisons are often uncertain. For example, it is not always possible to identify unique ICD codes for the NCCI injury classification codes and the OIICS nature of injury codes do not correspond one-to-one with WCIO recommended codes.

Portions of the individual records may be completed by parties unfamiliar with various coding systems which may lead to errors. For example, many employers may not know the codes for the nature of injury although online guides are available in many jurisdictions. Multi-source documents may be more prone to errors and omissions.

12. Loss Prevention

Many insurance carriers have loss prevention programs to identify and describe the particular risks that exist at policyholders' establishments, make recommendations for their abatement, and offer loss prevention[16] services to help policyholders manage these risks. They also assess risks that exist at establishments for which they contemplate underwriting new policies. For current policyholders, the primary purposes for the loss prevention services are to reduce the frequency and severity of workers' compensation claims and to improve the health and safety program of the client. Policyholders with higher premiums are more likely to receive routine loss prevention services from carriers than those with smaller premiums (Morin et al. 2013).

The provided services, which frequently are viewed as marketing tools to retain existing clients, may range from delivering relevant safety and health pamphlets and brochures to full risk characterizations that include recommendations for remediation with follow up inspections. Most small employers would not receive site visits unless their claims experience indicated a need for intervention.

Mandated Prevention Programs

All states have enacted legislation and developed related rules and regulations to reduce occupational injury and illness risks. The strategies employed by the states vary extensively and may include employer safety and health program requirements and incentives, insurance carrier loss prevention activities, registries of authorized occupational health and safety practitioners, and employer or organizational grants for risk mitigation and worker training (Table 3).[17] These inducements are often limited to those employers with greater than a minimum number of employees, minimum qualifying premiums, elevated experience modification factors, or that appear on lists of high hazard industries. Twelve states require workers' compensation insurance carriers to provide loss prevention services to many employers at no additional cost (Table 3). Requirement for these services is often limited to those policyholders with greater than a minimum number of employees, such as 25, or with premiums above minimum thresholds such as $25,000.

Carrier-Based Loss Prevention Programs

Most large workers' compensation insurance carriers invest portions of their revenues in loss prevention programs (Dembe 1995; Nave and Veltri 2004; Ryan 2013) although the amounts or percentages are not readily available. According to one recent report, 13% of large workers' compensation insurance clients, on average, receive loss control visits in a given year although that value varies widely by industry group (e.g. Manufacturing = 32%, Construction = 16%, Agriculture = 4%) (Ryan 2013). For the most part, loss prevention programs collect information on hazards and other determinants of risks from employers either prior to the issuance of a policy, i.e. risk selection for underwriting, or as a means of providing services to existing clients. Depending on the size of the premium, loss prevention services may include conduct of site visits which frequently include walk-through inspections of facilities, interviews with employees, supervisors and managers, as well as reviews of the employer's safety and health program elements. The report for the initial survey is shared with the carrier's underwriting staff as well as a broker that may be involved in the transaction. These risk selection reports are considered privileged information and often only selected portions of the reports are shared with the client (Morin et al. 2013).

For new and existing clients, key elements of loss prevention reports, such as a description of the hazards identified and recommendations for their abatement, may be provided to the employer. The loss prevention staff may also communicate the need for improvements (such as specific training or documentation) to the employer's health and safety programs. They may also provide specific services such as training employees, supervisors and managers and make training materials and model program elements available. Industrial hygiene and ergonomic surveys are included as needed. Afterwards, the loss prevention program may track progress through follow-up communications with the employer. The loss prevention professional may assist the employer in the completion of a safety grant application if they are available.

Loss prevention records are not standardized except perhaps within insurance providers. The availability of mobile technology applications for loss prevention programs is increasing and may provide additional opportunities for data standards developments on hazards and employer health and safety program elements.

13. Workers' Compensation Associations and Organizations

The workers' compensation insurance industry is supported by a large number of professional and trade associations and other organizations that operate at the international, national, state and even local levels. Some are membership organizations that provide professional services such as annual meetings, education and training. Some are research organizations that complete work under contracts. Others are affiliations of state and provincial agency representatives. Only a few of the longest-standing organizations will be mentioned here.

Two of the oldest workers' compensation insurance industry associations are NCCI and IAIABC. These organizations date from the earliest state workers' compensation programs in the U.S.

According to their Web site, NCCI "is the largest provider of workers' compensation and employee injury data and statistics in the nation." NCCI receives proprietary claims information from insurance carriers in their member states in the form of a Unit Statistical Data report which guides setting of manual rates for their client jurisdictions. To support the reporting system, NCCI in conjunction with WCIO has developed a number of standard coding schemes for nature of injury, event causation, and part-of-body. In addition, NCCI standard codes for industry, occupation and other factors are used by the nearly 40 affiliate jurisdictions. NCCI also conducts research and other analyses across a range of issues in the workers' compensation insurance industry. Many of their reports may be accessed at https://www.ncci.com/nccimain/pages/default.aspx.

The IAIABC mission statement is "to improve the efficiency and effectiveness of workers' compensation systems throughout the world." Among its published strategic principles are: "provide a forum for regulators, stakeholders and experts to share information and discuss issues and solutions; assist jurisdictions in identifying opportunities for reducing costs and improving the delivery of benefits; and develop, analyze, and promulgate standards and uniform practices." IAIABC has published a number of important insurance industry documents and it sponsors and supports the EDI. Much of their information may be accessed at http://www.iaiabc.org/i4a/pages/index.cfm?pageid=3277.

Other workers' compensation organizations include WCRI whose mission statement is: "to be a catalyst for significant improvements in workers' compensation systems, providing the public with objective, credible, high-quality research on important public policy issues." The institute is an independent and not-for-profit organization providing peer-reviewed, objective information about workers' compensation systems. Most of their documents are available to members only but some useful information may be found at http://www.wcrinet.org/about.html.

According to the NASI Web site, the academy is a nonprofit, nonpartisan and non-governmental organization led by the nation's experts on social insurance. It evaluates programs and data to develop solutions to challenges on social insurance and economic security. NASI supports research and publishes documents on social insurance topics and produces an annual report on workers' compensation programs in the U.S. that may be obtained free of charge at http://www.nasi.org/about.

WCIO "is a voluntary association of statutorily authorized or licensed rating, advisory, or data service organizations that collect workers compensation insurance information in one or more states." Members of the WCIO are managers of boards and agencies within the jurisdictions. Its forum supports development of electronic data transmission standards for insurers and rating/ advisory organizations. Additional information about WCIO and its range of products can be found at https://www.wcio.org/Document%20 Library/AboutPage.aspx.

ACORD is an international organization that facilitates the development of open consensus data standards and standard forms for many segments of the insurance industry, and works with its members and partner organizations to drive implementation of those standards. Their information may be found at http://www.acord. org/Pages/default.aspx.

A couple of other organizations that are widely recognized in the insurance industry include: John F. Burton Jr.'s Workers' Compensation Resource which provides access to data, research, and other information pertaining to workers' compensation in the United States and other countries when possible. The resource offers open access to many publications such as the 1972 Report of the National Commission on State Workmen's Compensation Laws. The extensive workers' compensation information may be found at http://workerscompresources.com/. Dr. Burton also hosts an annual meeting for discussion of current workers' compensation research.

The Liberty Mutual Research Institute for Safety (LMRIS) is a research organization funded by a private insurance company. For over 60 years, the institute has conducted scientifically rigorous, peer-reviewed research to improve worker safety and health. They conduct laboratory and field studies and publish records-based research using workers' compensation data collected by Liberty Mutual Insurance. Extensive information on LMRIS can be found at http://www.libertymutualgroup.com/omapps/ContentServer?page name=LMGroup/Views/LMG&ft=2&fid=1138356633468&ln=en

Other organizations that serve the workers' compensation insurance industry include the American Association of State Compensation Insurance Funds (AASCIF), American Insurance Association (AIA), National Association of Insurance Commissioners (NAIC), National Conference of Insurance Legislators (NCOIL), and Property and Casualty Insurers Association of America (PCIAA).

14. PUBLIC HEALTH RESEARCH AND SURVEILLANCE[18]

Public health is "the science and art of preventing disease, prolonging life and promoting health through the organized efforts and informed choices of society, organizations, public and private, communities and individuals" (Winslow 1920). Fundamentally, public health relies on surveillance programs to describe the distribution of disease and injury, detect new and emerging diseases and disorders, target intervention activities to prevent their incidence, and monitor the effectiveness of those interventions. Workers' compensation records may be used for public health research and surveillance activities. The terms "research" and "surveillance" have specific meaning in Federal public health activities which are briefly discussed here.

Research

Federal regulations state that "research means a systematic investigation, including research development, testing and evaluation, designed to develop or contribute to generalizable knowledge" (45 Code of Regulations (CFR) 46.102(d)). Investigators performing public health research or surveillance activities have the responsibility to ensure that the research is conducted in a manner consistent with legal and ethical requirements. All research involving human participants that is conducted or supported by the U.S. Department of Health and Human Services (DHHS) must comply with DHHS Policy for Protection of Human Research Subjects (45 CFR part 46). Investigators should consult with their local institutional review board for assistance with development of research or surveillance projects to insure that human subjects are appropriately protected.

Surveillance

Public health surveillance is the systematic, ongoing collection, management, analysis, and interpretation of data followed by the dissemination of these data to public health programs to stimulate public health action (Thacker et al. 2012). Surveillance systems can be used to monitor infectious and noninfectious diseases as well as injuries and deaths. Surveillance data can be primary in that they are collected for a specific public health purpose or they may be secondary in that the data were collected for other purposes yet they can be useful for tracking injuries, illnesses and deaths that occur in a defined population.

Occupational health surveillance is the tracking of workplace injuries, illnesses, hazards, and exposures. In the U. S., because there are no periodic national surveys of worker health, occupational health surveillance remains fragmented with substantial data gaps. However, the available surveillance data are used to guide efforts to improve worker safety and health and to monitor trends and progress over time (NIOSH 2013b). Data and information derived from surveillance can be used to:

1) guide immediate action for important cases;
2) measure the burden of an injury, disease, or other health-related event or exposure, including changes in related factors;
3) identify populations at risk, including new or emerging health concerns;
4) guide the planning, implementation, and evaluation of programs to prevent and control injuries, disease, or adverse exposures;
5) evaluate policies and practices;
6) detect changes in health practices and the effects of the changes;
7) prioritize the allocation of health resources;
8) describe the clinical course of disease; and
9) provide a basis for epidemiologic research.

Workers' compensation records, most commonly administrative claims data, are used for occupational surveillance. In some states, for example California (California Labor Code) and Washington (Department of Labor and Industries), workers' compensation claims information is used to identify more hazardous industries or leading events for claims across all industries. Claims information has been used to establish priorities for loss prevention and other intervention actions (Silverstein et al. 2002; Bonauto et al. 2006; Anderson et al. 2013). Yet other investigators have determined that workers' compensation claims data are currently inadequate to characterize occupational injuries and illnesses in particular (Rosenman et al. 2000; Azaroff et al. 2002; Utterback et al. 2012).

Formerly, workers' compensation claims information from a large number of states was collected by BLS for the Supplementary Data System (SDS), a nonrepresentative sample of occupational injuries and illnesses. SDS contained discrepancies due to the quality of data retrieved from states and the variability of state laws on which injuries and illnesses were reported

(National Research Council 1987). The system was discontinued in the late 1980's when the Survey of Occupational Injuries and Illnesses (SOII) along with the Census of Fatal Occupational Injuries (CFOI) were being developed.

Estimating Rates

Rates of occupational injuries and illnesses require estimates of at-risk populations (a "denominator"). The denominator commonly used in the workers' compensation industry is dollars of payroll. In public health, preferred denominators for rates are numbers of people or, in the case of occupational studies, full-time equivalent (FTE) workers. Data sets used to estimate the numbers of workers within industries and/or occupations may be obtained from population household surveys such as the Current Population Survey (CPS) or the American Community Survey (ACS), or from employer establishment survey programs such as Occupational Employment Statistics (OES), Current Employment Statistics (CES), or County Business Patterns (CBP). All of these data sources have broad coverage but exclude some types of workers. The Quarterly Census of Employment and Wages (QCEW), which is nearly comprehensive and collected by states for unemployment insurance purposes does report the number of workers by establishments although it does not distinguish between full-time and part-time workers. The QCEW data may be adjusted to estimate FTEs with hours per industry data from the surveys listed above. In any case, the scope, exclusions, and restrictions on survey and state level data should be carefully examined and understood.

15. Public Health Regulations

Many Federal, state and local government regulations have been developed to address public health concerns. It is beyond the scope of this document to describe the myriad public health concerns that are regulated. Instead, we limit this description to those authorities where workers' compensation data may be useful. The Occupational Safety and Health Administration (OSHA) and the Mine Safety and Health Administration (MSHA) are two Federal agencies with regulatory mandates to protect the health and safety of workers in the U.S. OSHA and MSHA regulations are available through their respective Web sites and elsewhere.[19, 20] Additionally, the US Environmental Protection Agency regulates pesticide hazards for agricultural workers.[21] State and local health departments are charged with protecting the health of all residents in their jurisdictions, and some health departments are active in workplace health and safety and tracking occupational illnesses and injuries. In fiscal year 2013, NIOSH provided funds to help support occupational health and safety surveillance programs in twenty-three states.[22]

Regulations are perceived by many as essential to the protection of public health. Individuals may not have the knowledge or resources that are required to make decisions about personal exposure to potentially hazardous materials including chemical, ergonomic, physical and biological agents. In the occupational arena, regulations are established by OSHA and MSHA to limit potential hazards through the use of interventions such as exposure limits, machine guarding, fall protection, trenching standards, medical screening and many more.

Regulations pertaining to workers' compensation are established by the individual jurisdictions including the states, territories, and the District of Columbia, and the Federal government for its own employees. The states frequently require all employers including those self-insured for workers' compensation to provide health and safety programs for their establishments. These requirements vary substantially across the jurisdictions and many are augmented by occupational safety and health requirements in departmen s of labor or similar agencies. Carrier-based loss prevention programs often assist employers in the recognition and control of hazards for which regulations apply. In addition to the insurance claims and medical information, records for these mandated activities may be useful for occupational safety and health research and surveillance.

16. Breaking through Barriers

Despite its limitations, research organizations, state-based surveillance programs, and workers' compensation agencies and associations have used claims data for research and surveillance purposes. Collaborations have been mostly within states due to problems with combining data from multiple jurisdictions. Additional collaborations would create further opportunities to use workers' compensation records and related information to prevent occupational injuries, illnesses and fatalities.

Overcoming some of the limitations would be possible with more systematic collection and analysis of workers' compensation data across industries and occupations. Further standardization of data elements and coding schemes such as universal adoption of ICD medical codes and ICD-E external cause of injury codes would be beneficial. Development of additional computer-based record systems would provide greater opportunities for more informative data collection and interpretation. Advances in auto-coding of data by computer systems, which rely on standard codes, would reduce the number of errors and missing data from the workers' compensation insurance records. Effective searching of unstructured text fields has also improved (Lehto et al. 2009; Patel et al. 2012; Bertke et al. 2013).

Although systematic data analysis within a carrier's operations contributes to risk management goals and client service, the information is not readily available to public health organizations. When made available, practitioners and researchers have used claims data for epidemiologic studies, to identify hazards, assess the effectiveness of controls, assign priorities for limited resources, and evaluate intervention programs.

Additional information on evaluations of workplace safety and health programs, hazard monitoring and hazard exposure data, and observations of worksites are types of loss prevention information that could be standardized and made more useful for research and surveillance purposes. Over the past century and more, carrier-based and state agency workers' compensation programs have used data to identify and evaluate risks for specific hazards across industry sectors.

When systematically available, workers' compensation data has been used extensively for occupational safety and health research and surveillance (NIOSH 2010; Utterback et al. 2012; NIOSH 2013a) and they have supplemented the surveillance information available from other occupational resources.[23] This primer provides background information for those interested in utilizing workers' compensation data for prevention purposes.

References

American Association of State Compensation Insurance Funds (2007). State Funds: Their Role in Workers' Compensation, (http://www.aascif.org /public/1.1.1 history.htm) Accessed on November 8, 2013.

Anderson NJ, Bonauto DK, Adams D (2013). Prioritizing Industries for Occupational Injury and Illness Prevention and Research, Washington State Workers' Compensation Claims Data, 2002- 2010. Washington State Department of Labor and Industries Technical Report Number 64-1-2013 (http://wwwini.wa.gov/Safety/Research/Files/bd_3F.pdf). Accessed on November 8, 2013.

Azaroff LS, Levenstein C, Wegman DH (2002). Occupational injury and illness surveillance: Conceptual filters explain underreporting. Am J Pub Health 92:1421-1429.

Bertke SJ, Meyers AR, Wurzelbacher SJ, Bell J, Lampl ML, Robins D (2012). Development and evaluation of a Naïve Bayesian model for coding causation of workers' compensation claims. J Safety Res 43(5-6):327-32.

Biddle J, Roberts K, Rosenman KD, Welch EM (1998). What percentage of workers with work-related illnesses receive workers' compensation benefits? J Occup Environ Med 40:325-331.

Boden LI, Biddle EA, Spieler EA (2001). Social and economic impacts of workplace illness and injury: Current and future directions for research. Am J Ind Med 40:398-402.

Boden L, Ozonoff A (2008). Capture-recapture estimates of nonfatal workplace injuries and illnesses. Annals Epidem 18:500-506.

Bonauto DK, Silverstein BA, Adams D, Foley M (2006). Prioritizing industries for occupational injury and illness prevention and research. J Occup Environ Med 48:840-851.

Burton JF (2004). A primer on workers' compensation, Workers' Compensation Policy Review. Nov/Dec 2004 (http://workerscomp resources.com/wp-content/uploads/2012/11/ND04A.pdf). Accessed November 7, 2013.

California Labor Code, Sections 6314.1, 6354 and 6355 (http://www.dir.ca.gov/doshpol/P&PC-19. html). Accessed on November 7, 2013

CDC (2010). Distinguishing public health research and public health nonresearch, CDCSA-2010-02, July 29, 2010 (http://www.cdc.gov /od/science/integrity/docs/cdc-policydistinguishing-public-health-research-nonresearch.pdf). Accessed November 7, 2013.

Cocchiarella L, Anderson GBJ, eds. (2001) Guides to the Evaluation of Permanent Impairment. 5th ed. Chicago, Ill: American Medical Association.

Courtney TK (2010). Workers' compensation data utilization in injury prevention research at the Liberty Mutual Research Institute for Safety. In: Proceedings of Use of Workers' Compensation Data for Occupational Injury and Illness Prevention. Utterback DF, Schnorr TM eds. Cincinnati, OH. National Institute for Occupational Safety and Health; DHHS (NIOSH) Pub No. 2010-152. pp. 49-53.

Dembe AE (1995). Alternative approaches for incorporating safety into state workers' compensation reform legislation. J Insurance Regulation 13:445-450.

Department of Health and Human Services, Health Information Privacy, (2003) Disclosures for Workers' Compensation Purposes 45 C.F.R. Sect. 164.512(l) (http://www.hhs.gov/ocr/privacy/ hipaa/understanding/coveredentities/workerscomp.html). Accessed on November 12, 2013.

Department of Health and Human Services (2013). Workers' compensation settlements and payments (http://www.medicare.gov/supplement-other-insurance/how-medicare-works-withother-insurance/who-pays-first/workers-comp-payments.html). Accessed on November 12, 2013

Environmental Protection Agency (2013). Worker Protection Standard for Agricultural Pesticides. (http://www.epa.gov/agriculture/twor.html). Accessed on November 12, 2013.

Fan ZJ, Bonauto DK, Foley MP, Silverstein BA (2006). Underreporting of work-related injury or illness to workers' compensation: individual and industry factors. J Occup Environ Med 48:914- 922.

Fishback PV (2013). Workers' Compensation. EH.net, (http://eh.net /encyclopedia/workerscompensation/). Accessed on November 12, 2013

Florida Division of Workers' Compensation (2012). 2011 Division of Workers' Compensation Annual Report. (http://www.myfloridacfo.com /wc/pdf/DWC-Annual-Report-2011.pdf). Accessed May 10, 2013

Guyton GP (1999). A Brief History of Workers' Compensation. Iowa Orthop J. 19: 106–110. (http://www.ncbi.nlm.nih.gov/pmc/articles/PMC 1888620/). Accessed on November 12, 2013.

Hakimzadeh S, Cohn D (2007). English usage among Hispanics in the United States, Pew Research Hispanic Center; Nov 29, 2007. (http://www.pewhispanic.org/2007/11/29/iv-workplaceand-home/). Accessed on November 7, 2013.

Hunt HA (2003-2004). Benefit adequacy in state workers' compensation programs. Social Security Bulletin. 65(4):24-30.

International Association of Industrial Accident Boards and Commissions (2004). A History of the IAIABC, 90th Annual Convention Edition http://www.iaiabc.org/files/Resources/2006HistoryofIAIABC.pdf. Accessed May 12, 2013

International Association of Industrial Accident Boards and Commissions (2013). EDI Implementation Guides. (http://www.iaiabc.org/i4a/pages /index.cfm?pageid=3339). Accessed on November 12, 2013.

Kiselica D, Sibson B, Green-McKenzie J (2004) Workers' compensation: a historical review and description of a legal and social insurance system. Clin Occup Environ Med. May;4(2):v, 237-47.

Lehto M, Marucci-Wellman H, Corns H (2009). Bayesian methods: A useful tool for classifying injury narratives into cause groups. Inj Prev Aug;15(4):259-65.

Leigh JP (2011). Economic burden of occupational injury and illness in the United States. Milbank Q 89:728-72.

Leigh JP, Marcin JP (2012). Workers' compensation benefits and shifting costs for occupational injury and illness. J Occup Environ Med 54:445-450.

Lipscomb HJ, Dement JM, Silverstein BA, Cameron W, Glazner JE (2009). Who is paying the bills? Health care costs for musculoskeletal back disorders, Washington State carpenters, 1989 – 2003. J Occup Environ Med 51:1185-1192.

Mine Health and Safety Administration (2013). Title 30 CFR Mineral Resources Parts 1 through 199. (http://www.msha.gov/30CFR /CFRINTRO.HTM). Accessed November 12, 2013.

Missouri Department of Labor and Industrial Relations (2012). Report of Injury. (http://labor. mo.gov/DWC/Forms/WC-1-EDI-AI.pdf). Accessed November 12, 2013.

Morin JF, Utterback DF, Shor G, Welsh L, Bogyo TJ, Wurzelbacher SJ (2013). Workers' compensation loss prevention information and interventions. Submitted for publication.

National Commission on State Workmen's Compensation Laws (1972). The Report of the National Commission on State Workmen's Compensation Laws. Washington DC: Government Printing Office. (http://www.workers compresources.com/National Commission Report/ national commission report.htm). Accessed on November 12, 2013.

National Research Council (1987). Counting injuries and illnesses in the workplace: Proposals for a better system. Pollack ES and Keimig DG eds. National Academy Press; Washington DC.

Nave M, Veltri A (2004). Effect of loss control services on reported injury incidents. J Safety Res 35:39-46.

NIOSH (2013a). Proceedings of Use of Workers' Compensation Data for Occupational Safety and Health, Utterback DF, Schnorr TM eds. Cincinnati, OH; National Institute for Occupational Safety and Health; DHHS (NIOSH) Pub No. 2013-147.

NIOSH (2013b). Topic Page: Surveillance Program. (http://www.cdc.gov /niosh/programs/surv/). Accessed November 7, 2013.

NIOSH (2010). Proceedings of Use of Workers' Compensation Data for Occupational Injury and Illness Prevention. Utterback DF, Schnorr TM eds. Cincinnati, OH. National Institute for Occupational Safety and Health; DHHS (NIOSH) Pub No. 2010-152.

Occupational Safety and Health Administration (2013). OSHA Law & Regulations. (http://www. osha.gov/law-regs.html). Accessed November 12, 2013.

Oklahoma Insurance Department (2013). Self-Funded Health Care Plans/Self-Insured Employers. (https://www.ok.gov/oid/Consumers/Insurance Basics /ERISA Information.html). Accessed November 7, 2013.

Oleinick A, Zaidman B (2004). Methodologic issues in the use of workers' compensation database for the study of work injuries with day away from work. I. Sensitivity of case ascertainment. Am J Ind Med 45:260-274.

Oregon (2013). 2012 Oregon Workers' Compensation Premium Rate Ranking Summary. (http:// actprod.cbs.state.or.us/iportal/report catalog.html). Accessed on November 7, 2013

O'Leary P, Boden LI, Seabury SA, Ozonoff A, Scherer E (2012). Workplace injuries and the take-up of Social Security disability benefits. Social Security Bulletin 72(3):1-17.

Ostbye T, Dement JM, Krause KM (2007). Obesity and workers' compensation: Results from the Duke Health and Safety Surveillance System. Arch Intern Med 167:766-73.

Patel MD, Rose KM, Owens CR, Bang H, Kaufman JS (2012). Performance of automated and manual coding systems for occupational data: A case study of historical records. Am J Ind Med 55(3):228-31.

Restrepo T, Shuford H (2011). Workers' compensation and the aging workforce. National Council on Compensation Insurance, Boca Raton, FL. (https://www.ncci.com/documents/2011 Aging Workforce Research Brief.pdf). Accessed on November 7, 2013.

Rosenman KD, Gardiner JC, Wang J, Biddle J, Hogan A, Reilly MJ, Roberts K, Welch E (2000). Why most workers with occupational repetitive trauma do not file for workers' compensation. J Occup Environ Med 42:25-34.

Ryan M (2013). Risk management and loss control industry trends. Presented at: E&S 2013 Loss Control Executive Forum, March 5, 2013 (http://www.iso.com/Conferences/Loss-Control-

Forum/Home.html?blogclick%20E&S%20Forum%20link). Accessed on November 7, 2013.

Scherzer T, Wolfe N (2008). Barriers to workers' compensation and medical care for injured personal assistance services workers. Home Health Care Serv Q 27:37-58.

Schmid F, Laws C, Montero M (2012). Indemnity benefit duration and obesity. National Council on Compensation Insurance, Boca Raton, FL. (https://www.ncci.com/documents/Obesity-2012.pdf). Accessed on November 7, 2013.

Sengupta I, Reno V, Burton JF, Baldwin M (2012). Workers' Compensation: Benefits, Coverage, and Costs, 2010, National Academy of Social Insurance, Washington DC.

Shuford H (2013). The role of professional employer organizations in workers compensation: Evidence of workplace safety and reporting. In: Proceedings of Use of Workers' Compensation Data for Occupational Safety and Health Workshop. Utterback DF, Schnorr TM eds. NIOSH Pub. No. 2013-147. pp. 51 – 56.

Shuford H, Restrepo T, Beaven N, Leigh JP (2009). Trends in components of medical spending within workers' compensation: Results from 37 states combined. J Occup Environ Med 51:232-238.

Silverstein BA, Viikari-Juntura E, Kalat J (2002). Use of a prevention index to identify injuries at high risk for work-related musculoskeletal disorders of the neck, back and upper extremity in Washington State. Am J Ind Med 41:149-169.

Smith CK, Silverstein BA, Bonauto DK, Adams D, Fan ZJ (2010). Temporary workers in Washington State. Am J Ind Med 53: 135-145.

Spieler E (1994). Perpetuating risk? Workers' compensation and the persistence of occupational injuries, 31 Houston Law Rev. 119-264. Excerpts reprinted in Employment Law (Rothstein M, Leibman L, eds.); 1995 Workers' Compensation Yearbook (Burton, JF Jr. ed. 1994).

Spieler EA, Burton JF (2012). The lack of correspondence between work-related disability and receipt of workers' compensation benefits. Am J Ind Med 55:487-505.

Spielholz P, Cullen J, Smith C, Howard N, Silverstein BA, Bonauto DK (2008). Assessment of perceived injury risks and priorities among truck drivers and trucking companies in Washington State. J Safety Res 39:569-576.

Thacker SB, Qualters JR, Lee LM (2012). Public health surveillance in the United States: Evolution and challenges. MMWR (Suppl) 61(03):3-9.

Thamann D, Reitz D (2000). Workers' Compensation Guide, Interpretation and Analysis, The National Underwriter Company, Cincinnati, OH.

Trogdon JG, Finkelstein EA, Hylands T, Dellea PS, Kamal-Bahl SJ (2008). Indirect costs of obesity: A review of the current literature. Obes Rev 9(5):489-500.

U.S. Bureau of Labor Statistics (2012). News Release: Nonfatal occupational injuries and illnesses requiring days away from work, 2011. Washington DC. November 8, 2012. (http://www.bls.gov/ news.release/osh2.nr0.htm). Accessed on June 11, 2013

U.S. Chambers of Commerce (2012). 2011 Analysis of Workers' Compensation Laws. Washington DC. (Updated annually in July of subsequent year)

Utterback DF, Schnorr TM, Silverstein BA, Spieler EA, Leamon TB, Amick BC (2012). Occupational health and safety surveillance and research using workers' compensation data. J Occup Environ Med 54:171-176.

Washington State Department of Labor and Industries (2012). Division of Occupational Safety and Health, Directive 2.10: Programmed inspection and visit activities, January 5, 2012. (http:// www.lni.wa.gov/Safety /Rules/Policies/PDFs/WRD210.pdf). Accessed on November 7, 2013.

Willborn SL, Schwab SJ, Burton JF, Lester GLL (2012). Employment Law: Cases and Materials. LexisNexis, New Providence, NJ.. p. 881.

Winslow, Charles-Edward Amory (1920). The untilled fields of public health. Science 51(1306): 23–33.

Wurzelbacher SJ, Meyers AR, Bertke SJ, Lampl M, Robins DR, Bushnell PT, Tarawneh A, Childress D, Turnes J (2013). Comparison of cost valuation methods for workers compensation. In: Proceedings of Use of Workers' Compensation Data for Occupational Safety and Health Workshop. Utterback DF, Schnorr TM eds. NIOSH Pub. No. 2013-147. pp.147-151.

Appendix A: Workers' Compensation Primer Glossary and Other Industry Terms

actuary – one who calculates insurance premiums, reserves and dividends

adjuster – see claims adjuster

appeal – right of an individual who received an adverse decision to seek review by a higher authority assigned risk – an insured entity that would normally be rejected by commercial insurance carriers in the voluntary market but is designated for coverage by state law

audit – examination and verification of employer records on payroll

basic premium – portion of a standard retrospective insurance premium that covers administrative costs, fees and commissions

broker – business that sells insurance coverage to employers; may represent a number of insurance carriers

captive – insurance provider for a single business organization that is owned by that organization

carrier – organization acting as an insurer

carve-outs – labor/management agreements for insurance coverage of occupational injuries and illnesses (has various other meanings in the insurance industry as a whole)

case manager – insurer representative that oversees medical treatments for injury or illness claims

claim – application for insurance benefits due to occupational injury or illness

claim disallowance – insurer rejection of a claim for medical treatment or indemnity costs

claimant – person making a demand for payment of benefits

claims adjuster – insurer representative who investigates claims for authenticity and settlements

claims initiator – person who completes the initial claim form for compensation

deductible – a type of workers' compensation insurance policy for which the initial loss to some specified limit is not reimbursed by insurance payment, i.e. the risk is retained by employer

disability – condition that curtails a person's ability to carry on normal pursuits

dividend plan – a type of workers' compensation insurance policy for which the insured may receive funds back (a dividend) if losses are less than anticipated

doctor's first report – initial claimant evaluation by physician which is required in some states

Electronic Data Interchange – developed several standard claim data reporting forms and was fostered by the IAIABC

exclusive funds – state-sponsored workers' compensation insurance in jurisdictions where private insurance is not allowed

exclusive remedy – in workers' compensation, the only recourse for worker injuries and illnesses experience modification factor – multiplier adjustment to employer's premium based on prior claims history in comparison with the average experience of the risk class, may be greater than or less than unity

first report of injury – initial form completed by claims initiator with detailed information on the claimant, employer, nature of injury, event description, and anticipated medical treatment needs

groups – similar industry employers that combine to share risks and insurance coverage; also may be employees that are covered under single insurance policy, e.g. group health insurance

guaranteed cost – a type of workers' compensation insurance policy where the premium is the only cost to the employer

impairment – alteration of an individual's health status; a deviation from normal in a body part or organ system and its functioning (Cocchiarella and Anderson 2001)

incurred losses – paid plus reserved claim costs, including medical and indemnity; experience modification ratings are based on incurred costs

indemnity payments – compensation for lost work time claim paid to covered injured or ill workers to partially replace lost wages

independent medical examiner – registered medical practitioners who provide impartial medical assessments

loss control – see loss prevention

loss development factor – prediction of future payments on open claims

loss prevention – actions to limit risk through hazard recognition and abatement and safety and health program evaluation; also known as loss control

loss ratio – insured losses divided by premiums earned in a given period

loss reduction – activities to limit financial losses and disability after a claim is filed for an injury or illness; also known as medical or disability management

loss runs – employer-based information on prior claims experience lost work days – accrual of time away from work due to an occupational injury or illness

managed care – enrolled medical services that focuses on care utilization and costs

manual rate – published rates, established by rating bureaus, for insured groups based on average costs for the group

medical only claim – workers' compensation claim for medical treatment expenses and does not include lost work days meeting the minimum lost time requirement for indemnity payments medical review board – state sanctioned group of medical practitioners that provides independent medical expertise on appropriate treatments, disability determination, and other science-based criteria

Medicare set-aside – allocation in a claim settlement to pay future medical expenses that would have been paid by Medicare

monopolistic funds – see exclusive funds

mutual insurance company – organization that issues insurance policies and is owned by its policyholders

net premium – total insurance premium after adjustments for experience modification and discounts

pools – multiple meanings but usually a collection of groups that share insurance coverage

professional employer organization (PEO) – firm that hires a client company's employees, becoming the policy holder of record for workers' compensation; this arrangement results in co-employment

pure premium – portion of manual rate that covers anticipated losses and loss adjustment expenses

rating bureau – state sanctioned private group that establishes permitted manual rates for insurance premiums

reciprocal group – association of employer entities that mutually share risks of economic losses

re-insurance – insurance purchased by an insurance carrier to limit risks

reserve funds – accounting liability for the current value of future expected costs on a claim

residual market – portion of employers unable to obtain insurance coverage in the voluntary market

retrospective rating – a type of workers' compensation insurance policy where the premium is based on the actual insured losses during the policy term

return-to-work – program to assist injured workers regain employment after a claim has been filed

risk group – see groups

risk retention – portion of possible future liability that is not covered by an insurance policy

scheduled benefit – pre-determined amount of payment for specified loss such as an amputation

Second Injury Fund – insurance provided for previously disabled workers

self-insured – a type of workers' compensation insurance policy where the employer is responsible for its own losses associated with required risk coverage single payer – for health insurance, a single entity, generally a government agency, is responsible for all insured costs

state funds – state government offered mandatory insurance; may be exclusive (monopolistic) in a few states or competitive in yet other states

subrogation – recovery of claim expenses from another responsible party

Supplemental Data System – survey of workers' compensation claims information by Bureau of Labor Statistics in the 1970's and 1980's prior to the Survey of Occupational Injuries and Illnesses and the Census of Fatal Occupational Injuries

surety bond – financially backed guarantee to reimburse third party losses

surveillance – ongoing systematic collection, analysis, and interpretation of health data essential to the planning, implementation, and evaluation of public health practices, closely integrated with the timely dissemination of these data to those who need to know

third-party administrator – insurance businesses that provide services to employers, brokers, insurers, and groups related to workers' compensation claims

underwriter – one who selects risks to be solicited or rates the acceptability of risks

underwriting – to be responsible for financial losses in accordance with an insurance policy

uninsured employer fund – state funds to cover losses when employer has failed to obtain required insurance

Unit Statistical Report – information on workers' compensation loss experiences reported to a rating agency

value – estimates of current or future liability costs on a claim

voluntary market – competitive market for workers' compensation insurance that exists in all but the 4 exclusive fund states

APPENDIX B: PREPARING FOR ENGAGEMENT

In preparation for contacting the workers' compensation data custodian, one should consider several issues and evaluate some available resources. For example, one should visit the Web site for the workers' compensation program in the state to evaluate the available information such as annual reports and reporting forms. In addition, the Web sites have links to applicable statutes and regulations with explanatory guides for injured workers and their employers. Researchers and public health practitioners may also want to think about the issues below prior to approaching potential collaborating organizations who are workers' compensation data custodians. If the state workers' compensation Web sites does not provide specific information on their requirements, these issues may be addressed in direct communications with a knowledgeable agency official.

Study Background Questions

What are the proposed project concept and time commitments? Might provide examples from other jurisdictions

- Surveillance – ongoing analysis of longitudinal data
- Etiologic research – may be time limited relationship but usually longitudinal data

What data sources may be needed for the project?

- Public agencies – do they have a research unit or other organization with shared interest/ mission?
- Private – if restricted, can they share de-identified data, are they comprehensive?

Are there specific legal restrictions on data availability from state agencies?

Can data be examined or explored prior to collaboration commitment?

What are the possible mutual benefits for the collaborating organizations?

- Examine their existing products
- Review examples from other jurisdictions (e.g. Florida Annual Report)
- Reinforce experience with confidential handling of personal and other sensitive information
- Think about realistic needs for future information, assistance and review

How are data stored and what formats are used?

- Electronic: on line or downloaded (CD, DVD, hard drives, encryption?)
- Hard copy
- Incomplete data and historical gaps in data
- Denominator (population) data available for rate estimation (unemployment insurance agencies)?

Which, if any, standardized data coding systems and which versions are used (e.g. WCIO, OIICS, NCCI, NAICS, ICD E-codes)?

Is a data dictionary available?

Are narrative fields part of the records that may require data mining?

What are the proposed agreements for clearance of articles, reports and other products?

Other State Coverage Questions

If the state publishes an annual report, what kind of information is captured in the report?

What exclusion criteria are used to decide which employers need to provide workers' compensation coverage for workers? For example

- Minimum employer size*
- Industry sector (e.g. agriculture)*
- Familial relationship of the employee with the employer*
- Self-employed workers*
- Corporate officers*

Are separate rules written for industries such as agriculture, construction or mining? Does the state offer workers' compensation insurance plans? If yes, for which employers? Which employers, if any, are allowed to self-insure in the state?*

Does NCCI or another rating bureau collect standardized data from insurance carriers in the state?

Does the state require private insurance companies to write coverage for residual market employers?

Are employers in the state allowed to form groups or pools to obtain insurance in the voluntary markets?

Are employers in the state allowed to combine to create a self-insured entity?

Are carve-out arrangements permitted in the state?

What automatic, Web-based or telemetric reporting systems are used in the state?

Who can file a first report of injury?

What requirements exist related to managed care organizations in the state?*

What requirements govern the choice of treating physicians in the state?*

What requirements exist related to vocational rehabilitation in the state?*

What requirements restrict treatment options in the state?*

Has the state imposed any time or cost limits on compensation for disabled workers? If yes, what are they?*

*Answers to these questions can be found in the annual "Analysis of Workers' Compensation Laws" produced by U.S. Chambers of Commerce

End Notes

[1] More on the exclusion of workers' compensation medical records from the HIPAA Privacy Rule can be found at http://www.hhs.gov/ocr/privacy/hipaa/understanding /coveredentities /workerscomp.html

[2] This document uses "requirements" as a substitute term for legislation, statutes, rules and regulations since the sources for the legal obligations vary among the states.

[3] References to state workers' compensation laws in this document should be read to include the territories of Guam and the Virgin Islands plus the District of Columbia, all of which have separate statutes and regulations.

[4] For greater details on the history and development of workers' compensation laws in Europe and the U.S., readers are directed to http://www.iaiabc.org/files/Resources/2006HistoryofIAIABC.pdf, http://eh.net/encyclopedia/workers-compensation/, http://www.ncbi.nlm.nih.gov /pmc /articles /PMC 1888620/, or http://www.aascif.org/public/1.1.1 history.htm

[5] For greater details on workers' compensation trends and individual state requirements, readers are directed to the annual NASI report (Sengupta et al. 2012) and the annual report produced by the U.S. Chambers of Commerce (U.S. Chamber of Commerce 2012).

[6] The classifications do not directly correspond to Standard Industry Classification (SIC) or NAICS codes or occupational classification systems, such as the Standard Occupation Classes (SOC).

[7] http://www.workerscompresources.com/National Commission Report/national commission report.htm

[8] http://www.ncbi.nlm.nih.gov/pubmed/15182746, http://www.ssa.gov/policy/docs/ssb /v65n4/v65n4p24.pdf http://www.workerscompresources. com/, National Commission Report/National Commission/1-2004/Jan2004 nat com.htm

[9] Medicaid set-asides for occupational injuries and illnesses are explained at http://www.medicare. gov/supplement-other-insurance/how-medicare-works-with-other-insurance/who-pays-first/ workers-comp-payments.html.

[10] "Carve out" has different meanings across the insurance industry. The definition used for workers' compensation insurance carve outs in California may be found at http://www.dir. ca.gov/dwc/carveout.html.

[11] Burton's Workers' Compensation Resource provides access to a wide range of relevant materials. http://workerscompresources.com/wp-content/uploads/2012/11/ND04A.pdf

[12] One example of an EDI FROI can be found at http://labor.mo.gov/DWC/Forms/WC-1-EDI-AI.pdf.

[13] set of slides that explain unit reporting is available at http://www.ncci.com/documents/DRW-2008-Unit-Data-Reporting.pdf

[14] NCCI's Statistical Plan for Workers Compensation and Employers Liability is applicable in Alaska, Alabama, Arizona, Arkansas, Colorado, Connecticut, District of Columbia, Florida, Georgia, Hawaii, Idaho, Illinois, Indiana, Iowa, Kansas, Kentucky, Louisiana, Maine, Maryland, Mississippi, Missouri, Montana, Nebraska, Nevada, New Hampshire, New Mexico, Oklahoma, Oregon, Rhode Island, South Carolina, South Dakota, Tennessee, Utah, Vermont, Virginia and West Virginia.

[15] http://www.iaiabc.org/i4a/pages/index.cfm?pageid=3339

[16] Note that "loss control" and "loss prevention" are terms that are often used interchangeably. In contrast, the term "loss reduction" is typically used to refer to the management of costs and disability once an injury or illness has occurred through programs such as case management and return-to-work.

[17] States that do not appear in Table 3 list of prevention requirements or incentives are Alaska, Arizona, Georgia, Idaho, Indiana, Iowa, Kentucky, Maryland, Michigan, New Jersey, South Carolina, Vermont, Virginia and West Virginia

[18] For a thorough explanation of public health research and non-research as defined by CDC, please see http://www.cdc.gov/od/science/integrity/docs/cdc-policy-distinguishing-public-healthresearch-nonresearch.pdf .

[19] http://www.osha.gov/law-regs.html

[20] http://www.msha.gov/30CFR/CFRINTRO.HTM

[21] http://www.epa.gov/agriculture/twor.html

[22] The NIOSH funded surveillance programs in 2013 exist in the following states: California, Colorado, Connecticut, Florida, Georgia, Illinois, Iowa, Kentucky, Louisiana, Maryland, Massachusetts, Michigan, Minnesota, Nebraska, New Hampshire, New Jersey, New Mexico, New York, North Carolina, Oregon, Texas, Washington, and Wisconsin.

[23] Descriptions of many data sources used for occupational surveillance may be accessed at http:// wwwn.cdc.gov/niosh-survapps/Gateway/DataSources.aspx.

In: Workers' Compensation Insurance
Editor: Emmanuel Sanford
ISBN: 978-1-63117-651-7

Chapter 2

THE FEDERAL EMPLOYEES' COMPENSATION ACT (FECA): WORKERS' COMPENSATION FOR FEDERAL EMPLOYEES*

Scott Szymendera

SUMMARY

The Federal Employees' Compensation Act (FECA) is the workers' compensation program for federal employees. Like all workers' compensation programs, FECA pays disability, survivors, and medical benefits, without fault, to employees who are injured or become ill in the course of their federal employment and the survivors of employees killed on the job. The FECA program is administered by the Department of Labor (DOL) and the costs of benefits are paid by each employee's host agency. Employees of the U.S. Postal Service (USPS) currently comprise the largest group of FECA beneficiaries and are responsible for the largest share of FECA benefits.

Elements of the FECA program include

* This is an edited, reformatted and augmented version of Congressional Research Service Publication, No. R42107, dated June 4, 2013.

- basic disability benefits equal to two-thirds of an injured worker's pre-disability wage, which rises to 75% of the pre-disability wage if the worker has any dependents;
- disability benefits that continue for the duration of disability or the life of the beneficiary and in cases of traumatic injuries, beneficiaries can receive a continuation of their full pay for the first 45 days;
- disability benefits for persons with specific permanent partial disabilities, such as the loss of a limb, for a set number weeks provided by schedules set by statute and regulation;
- all medical costs associated with covered conditions without any copayments, cost-sharing, or use of private insurance by the beneficiaries;
- cash benefits for the survivors of employees killed on the job based on the worker's wages and a modest benefit for funeral costs; and
- vocational rehabilitation services to assist beneficiaries in returning to work.

This report also focuses on several key policy issues facing the program, including the disproportionate share of claims and program costs attributed to postal workers, the payment of FECA benefits after retirement age, the overall level of FECA disability benefits as compared with those offered by the states, and the administration of the FECA program.

The modern FECA program can trace its roots to 1916 but has not been significantly amended since 1974. A legislative history of the FECA program is provided in the Appendix.

INTRODUCTION

The Federal Employees' Compensation Act (FECA) is the workers' compensation system for federal employees. Every civilian employee of the federal government, including employees of the executive, legislative, and judicial branches, is covered by FECA, as are several other groups, including federal jurors and Peace Corps volunteers. In FY2009, the FECA program paid out more than $2.7 billion in benefits, including $1.8 billion in disability benefits, $847 million in medical benefits, and $138 million in benefits to the survivors of federal employees killed on the job.[1] In FY2009, administrative expenses made up 4.9% of total program costs.[2]

OVERVIEW OF THE FECA PROGRAM

Statutory and Regulatory Authorities

The FECA program is authorized in statute at 5 U.S.C. Sections 8101 *et seq*. Regulations implementing the FECA are provided at 20 C.F.R. Sections 10.00-10.826. The FECA program is administered by the Department of Labor, Office of Workers' Compensation Programs (OWCP).

Program Financing

Benefits under FECA are paid out of the federal Employees' Compensation Fund. This fund is financed by appropriations from Congress that are used to pay current FECA benefits and that are ultimately reimbursed by federal agencies through the chargeback process.

Each quarter OWCP provides to all federal agencies with employees receiving FECA benefits an estimate of the cost of these benefits to assist these agencies in preparing their budget requests. By August 15 of each year, OWCP sends each agency a statement of their FECA costs for the previous fiscal year. Each agency must include in its next budget request an appropriation to cover its FECA costs for the previous fiscal year. Upon receiving this appropriation, or if a non-appropriated entity of the government, by October 15, the agency must reimburse the Employees' Compensation Fund for the costs of the FECA benefits provided to its employees.

The administrative costs associated with the FECA program are provided to the DOL through the appropriations process. In addition, the USPS and certain other non-appropriated entities of the federal government are required to pay for the "fair share" of the costs of administering benefits for their employees. In 2010, the USPS paid approximately $61 million in FECA administrative costs.[3]

FECA Benefit and Administrative Costs

Table 1 provides data on the costs of providing FECA compensation and medical benefits as well as administrative costs associated with the FECA program. In FY2010, compensation benefits made up 68.4% of the nearly $2.9 billion in total FECA benefits and direct administrative costs made up 5.1% of total program costs.[4]

Table 1. FECA Benefits, FY2010

	Cost (in thousands of dollars)	**Percentage of Total Benefit Costs**
Compensation Benefits	1,976,439	68.4
Medical Benefits	912,882	31.6
Total Benefits	2,889,321	100.0

Source: Ishita Sengupta, Virginia Reno, and John F. Burton, Jr., *Workers' Compensation: Benefits, Coverage, and Costs, 2010*, National Academy of Social Insurance, Washington, DC, August 2012, p. 81.

Employees Covered by FECA

The FECA program covers all civilians employed by the federal government, including employees in the executive, legislative, and judicial branches of the government. Both full-time and part-time workers are covered, as are most volunteers and all persons serving on federal juries. Coverage is also extended to certain groups, including state and local law enforcement officers acting in a federal capacity, federal jurors, Peace Corps volunteers, students participating in Reserve Officer Training Corps programs, and members of the Coast Guard Auxiliary and Civil Air Patrol.

Conditions Covered by FECA

Under FECA, workers' compensation benefits are paid to any covered employee for any disability or death caused by any injury or illness sustained during the employee's work for the federal government. There is no list of covered conditions nor is there a list of conditions that are not covered. However, no injury, illness, or death may be compensated by FECA if the condition was

- caused by the willful misconduct of the employee;
- caused by the employee's intention to bring about the injury or death of himself or another person; or
- proximately caused by the intoxication of the employee.

In addition, any person convicted of a felony related to the fraudulent application for or receipt of FECA benefits forfeits his or her rights to all FECA benefits for any injury that occurred on or before the date of conviction. The benefits of any person confined in jail, prison, or an institution pursuant to a felony conviction are suspended for the duration of the incarceration and may not be recovered.

FECA Claims Process

All FECA claims are processed and adjudicated by OWCP. Initial decisions on claims are made by OWCP staff based on evidence submitted by the claimant and his or her treating physician. The law also permits OWCP to order a claimant or beneficiary to submit to a medical examination from a doctor contracted to the federal government. An employee dissatisfied with a claims decision may request a hearing before OWCP or an OWCP review of the record of its decision. A final appeal can be made to the Employees' Compensation Appeals Board (ECAB). The decision of the ECAB is final, cannot be appealed, and is not subject to judicial review.

Time Limit for Filing FECA Claims

In general, a claim for disability or death benefits under FECA must be made within three years of the date of the injury or death. In the case of a latent disability, such as a condition caused by exposure to a toxic substance over time, the three-year time limit does not begin until the employee is disabled and is aware, or reasonably should be aware, that the disability was caused by his or her employment.

FECA Compensation Benefits

Continuation of Pay

In the case of a traumatic injury, an employee is eligible for continuation of pay.[5] Continuation of pay is paid by the employing agency and is equal to 100% of the employee's rate of pay at the time of the traumatic injury. Since continuation of pay is considered salary and not compensation, it is taxed and subject to any deductions normally made against the employee's salary. Any lost work time beyond 45 days, or lost time due to a latent condition, is considered either a partial or total disability under FECA.

Employees of the United States Postal Service must satisfy a three-day waiting period before becoming eligible for continuation of pay.

Partial Disability

If an employee is unable to work full-time at his or her previous job, but is able to work either part-time or at a job in a lower pay category, then he or she is considered partially disabled and eligible for the following compensation benefits:

- if the employee is single, a monthly benefit equal to two-thirds of the difference between the employee's pre-disability and post-disability monthly wage or
- if the employee has at least one dependent, a monthly benefit equal to 75% of the difference between the employee's pre-disability and post-disability monthly wage.

The compensation benefits paid for partial disability are capped at 75% of the maximum basic pay at rate GS-15 (GS-15, step 10), are not subject to federal taxation, and are subject to an annual cost-of-living adjustment. Benefits are paid for the duration of the disability or the life of the beneficiary.

If an employee's actual wages do not accurately represent his or her true wage-earning capacity, or if he or she has no wages, then his or her partial disability benefit is based on his or her wage-earning capacity as determined by OWCP using a combination of vocational factors and "degree of physical impairment."

Scheduled Benefits

In cases in which an employee suffers a permanent partial disability, such as the loss of a limb, he or she is entitled to a scheduled benefit. The scheduled benefit is in addition to any other partial or total disability benefits received. An employee may receive a scheduled award even if he or she has returned to full-time work.[6] The list of scheduled benefits is provided in the **Appendix A** to this report. If an employee suffers a disfigurement of the face, head, or neck that is of such severity that it may limit his or her ability to secure or retain employment, the employee is entitled to up to $3,500 in additional compensation.

Total Disability

If an employee is unable to work at all, then he or she is considered totally disabled and eligible for the following compensation benefits:

- if the employee is single, a monthly benefit equal to two-thirds of the employee's pre-disability monthly wage or
- if the employee has at least one dependent, a monthly benefit equal to 75% of the employee's pre-disability monthly wage.

The compensation benefits paid for total disability are capped at 75% of the maximum basic pay at rate GS-15 (GS-15, step 10), are not subject to federal taxation, and are subject to an annual cost-of-living adjustment. Benefits are payable until it is determined that the employee is no longer totally disabled and may continue until the employee's death.

Death

If an employee dies on the job or from a latent condition caused by his or her employment, the employee's survivors are eligible for the following compensation benefits:

- if the employee's spouse has no children, then the spouse is eligible for a monthly benefit equal to 50% of the employee's monthly wage at the time of death or
- if the employee's spouse has one or more children, then the spouse is eligible for a monthly benefit equal to 45% of the employee's monthly wage at the time of death and each child is eligible for a monthly benefit equal to 15% of the employee's monthly wage at the time of death, up to a maximum family benefit of 75% of the employee's monthly wage at the time of death.

Special rules apply in cases in which an employee dies without a spouse or children or with only children.

If a spouse remarries before the age of 55, then he or she is entitled to a lump-sum payment equal to 24 months of benefits, after which all benefits cease. If a spouse remarries at the age of 55 or older, benefits continue for life. A child's benefits end at the age of 18, or age 23 if the child is still in school. A child's benefits continue for life if the child is disabled and incapable of self-support.

The compensation benefits paid for death are capped at 75% of the maximum basic pay at rate GS-15, are not subject to federal taxation, and are subject to an annual cost-of-living adjustment.

Additional Death Benefits

The personal representative of the deceased employee is entitled to reimbursement, up to $200, of any costs associated with terminating the deceased employee's formal relationship with the federal government. The personal representative of the deceased employee is also entitled to a reimbursement of funeral costs up to $800, and the federal government will pay any costs associated with shipping a body from the place of death to the employee's home. An employee killed while working with the military in a contingency operation is also entitled to a special gratuity payment of up to $100,000 payable to his or her designated survivors.

FECA Medical Benefits

Under FECA, all medical costs—including medical devices, therapies, and medications— associated with the treatment of a covered injury or illness are paid for, in full, by the federal government. A FECA beneficiary is not responsible for any coinsurance or any other costs associated with his or her medical treatment and does not have to use any personal insurance for any covered medical costs. A published fee schedule is used by OWCP to determine the rate or reimbursement paid to medical providers.[7]

Generally, a beneficiary may select his or her own medical provider and is reimbursed for the costs associated with transportation to receive medical services. Medical providers must be authorized by OWCP and can have their authorization removed if it is determined that they are violating program rules or are involved in fraud.

A FECA beneficiary who is blind, paralyzed, or otherwise disabled such that he or she needs constant personal attendant care may receive an additional benefit of up to $1,500 per month.

Vocational Rehabilitation

The Secretary of Labor may direct any FECA beneficiary to participate in vocational rehabilitation, the costs of which are paid by the federal government. While participating in vocational rehabilitation, the beneficiary may receive an additional benefit of up to $200 per month. However, any beneficiary who is directed to participate in vocational rehabilitation and fails to do so may have his or her benefit reduced to a level consistent with the increased wage earning capacity that likely would have resulted from participation in vocational rehabilitation.

Coordination with Other Benefits

Coordination with Retirement Benefits for Federal Employees

Most federal employees are covered by either the Civil Service Retirement System (CSRS) or the Federal Employees' Retirement System (FERS).[8] The CSRS covers federal employees initially hired before January 1, 1984. The FERS covers employees hired on or after that date and CSRSeligible employees who voluntarily switched to FERS coverage during "open seasons" held in 1986 and 1987. Employees contribute to the cost of the CSRS and FERS through payroll taxes. Both the CSRS and FERS provide for defined benefit pensions for retired and disabled federal employees. The FERS defined benefit pension is smaller than that provided by the CSRS, however, the FERS also provides for participation in the Social Security system and the Thrift Savings Plan (TSP), a federally managed defined contribution plan similar to a 401(k) plan offered to private-sector workers.[9]

While an injured federal employee is receiving FECA benefits and not working, he or she does not make any CSRS or FERS contributions, but does continue to accrue time in service for the purposes of retirement eligibility.[10] Because FECA benefits are not considered earnings under either the Social Security Act or Internal Revenue Code, FECA beneficiaries generally may not contribute to the Social Security system via the payroll tax or to the TSP.

Once a FECA beneficiary becomes eligible for CSRS or FERS retirement benefits, he or she may elect to receive these retirement benefits or remain in the FECA program for the duration of disability. Once this election is made, it may be changed at any time.

That amount of the FERS basic annuity is increased from 1% of the employee's high-three average pay to 2% of the high-three average pay for any period during which the employee was receiving FECA benefits rather than earnings. This provision, enacted in 2003, is designed to partially replace retirement income lost because of the employee's inability to contribute to the Social Security system or the TSP while receiving FECA benefits.[11]

Coordination with Disability Retirement Benefits

Both the CSRS and FERS offer federal employees who are unable to continue working because of disabilities the option to take a disability retirement annuity before reaching normal retirement age.[12] For the purposes of the CSRS and FERS disability retirement systems, an employee is considered disabled and eligible for an annuity if he or she is unable to perform his or her current federal job and cannot be accommodated with a job at the same rate of pay by his or her employing-agency because of a medical condition that is expected to last at least one year. An employee must have five years of service to qualify for disability retirement benefits under CSRS and 18 months of service under FERS. Generally, the amount of an employee's disability annuity is lower than what the employee would have received had he or she worked until normal retirement age and collected a CSRS or FERS retirement annuity.

As in the cases of a FERS or CSRS retirement annuity, a FECA beneficiary who is also eligible for CSRS or FERS disability retirement benefits may elect to receive these disability retirement benefits or remain in the FECA program for the duration of disability. Once this election is made, it may be changed at any time.

Coordination with Social Security Disability Insurance Benefits

Because FECA is a workers' compensation program, it is covered by the public disability offset provisions of Section 224 of the Social Security Act.[13] If a FECA beneficiary is also receiving Social Security Disability Insurance (SSDI) benefits, then the total amount of the beneficiary's monthly SSDI benefit, all SSDI benefits paid to his or her spouse or dependents, and his or her FECA benefit cannot exceed 80% of his or her average monthly wage at the time of his or her disability.[14] The FECA beneficiary's SSDI benefits, or the benefits for his or her spouse or dependents, are reduced until the 80% threshold is reached.

Coordination with Social Security Retirement Benefits

Federal employees covered by the FERS system are also covered by the Social Security system for their periods of federal employment. If a federal employee covered by FERS is entitled to both FECA and Social Security retirement benefits, the amount of his or her monthly FECA benefit is reduced by the amount of his or her Social Security retirement benefit attributable to his or her federal service.

SELECT CURRENT ISSUES FACING THE FECA PROGRAM

In recent years, Congress and the President have focused their attention on various issues facing the FECA program. There was significant legislative activity regarding FECA program reform in both the House and Senate in the 112th Congress. As part of larger U.S. Postal Service (USPS) reform legislation, the House Committee on Oversight and Government Reform reported legislation (H.R. 2309) that would have made changes to the FECA program as it applies to postal workers. The Senate passed legislation (S. 1789) that would have made significant reforms to the FECA program for all federal employees. The main vehicle for FECA program reform in the House was H.R. 2465, which was passed by the House and which would have made changes to the FECA program for all federal employees. Similar legislation is expected to be taken up during the 113th Congress.

The President has included FECA reform proposals in his FY2012, FY2013, and FY2014 Budgets. The President's FY2014 FECA reform proposal includes a lower base rate of FECA compensation, reduced benefits at retirement age to encourage beneficiaries to convert to federal retirement benefits, a requirement that all agencies pay their "fair share" of program administrative costs, and provisions that address program integrity and ongoing management of disability cases.[15]

FECA and the U.S. Postal Service

The USPS and its employees make up the largest component of the FECA program, and postal workers are injured on the job at rates disproportionate to the rest of the federal government. As shown in **Table 2**, although postal workers make up 21.5% of the federal workforce, they are responsible for 39.3% of injuries, illnesses, and fatalities that resulted in FECA cases in FY2012.[16]

The most significant area in which the experience of the USPS with the FECA program differs from that of the rest of the government is in the severity and duration of injuries and illnesses that result in FECA cases. As shown in **Table 3**, in FY2010, injuries and illnesses to postal workers resulted in 218.7 lost production days per 100 employees, compared with 77.4 days for the entire federal government and 34.8 days for non-postal federal entities.[17] This means that for every one of the 593,850 postal workers, more than two days of work were lost due to injuries, illnesses, or fatalities and that an estimated total of 1,298,750 production days, or 4,995 work years at the USPS were lost in FY2010 due to injuries, illnesses, and fatalities.[18]

Table 2. FECA Cases, FY2012

	Employees[a]		FECA Cases[b]		
Category	Total	Percentage	Total	Percentage	Per 100 Employees
Federal Government	2,829,998	100.0	97,238	100.0	3.4
U.S. Postal Service	607,814	21.5	38,206	39.3	6.3
Federal Government, excluding U.S. Postal Service	2,222,184	78.5	59,032	60.7	2.7

Source: Congressional Research Service (CRS) table with data taken from Department of Labor, Occupational Safety and Health Administration, *Federal Injury and Illness Statistics for Fiscal Year 2012,* http://www.osha.gov/dep/fap/statistics /fedprgms_stats12_final.html.

Note: Numbers may not add due to rounding and the number of federal employees calculated at different times during the year.

[a] Average number of employees during period from December 2011 through March 2012.

[b] Includes all new injury, illness, and fatality cases submitted to FECA, less any denied claims.

The USPS was the only federal entity with more than 200 lost production days per 100 employees in FY2010, and in FY2010 the only two other entities that had at least 150 lost production days were the Armed Forces Retirement Home and the International Boundary and Water Commission, small entities with approximately 250 employees each. The USPS in FY2010 was responsible for 60% of the total number of lost production days by the entire federal government.

Given the disproportionate number of injuries and lost production days attributed to the USPS, it is not surprising that benefits for postal workers make up a disproportionate share of the total costs of the FECA program. In chargeback year 2009, the FECA program paid approximately $2.7 billion in total benefits, with nearly $1.1 billion in benefits, or 40% of total benefits, being paid for claims by postal workers.[19]

As discussed earlier in this report, in 2006, with the enactment of P.L. 109-435, Congress changed the application of the three-day waiting period for postal workers with traumatic injuries with the goal of reducing FECA costs to the USPS. Under this provision, postal workers now must satisfy the three-day FECA waiting period before the beginning of the continuation of pay period, rather than after this period and before receiving FECA compensation.

Table 3. Lost Time FECA Cases and Lost Production Days due to Injuries, Illnesses, and Deaths, FY2010

	Lost Time Cases			
Category	Total Cases	Percentage of Total Federal Cases	Cases Per 100 Employees	Estimated Lost Production Days Per 100 Employees
Federal Government	47,226	100.0	1.68a	77.4a
U.S. Postal Service	15,311	32.4	2.58b	218.7b
Federal Government, excluding U.S. Postal Service	31,915	67.6	1.44c	34.8c

Source: The Congressional Research Service (CRS) with data taken from Department of Labor, Occupational Safety and Health Administration, Federal Injury and Illness Statistics for Fiscal Year 2010, http://www.osha.gov/ dep/fap/statistics /fedprgms_stats10_final.html; and Department of Labor, Office of Workers' Compensation Programs, FY2010 End of Year LPD Report for All Government, http://www.dol.gov/owcp/dfec/share/lpd/ FY20104thQtr/All Government.htm.

Note: Numbers may not add due to rounding and the number of federal employees calculated at different times during the year.

[a] Based on 2,804,206 employees in June 2010.

[b] Based on 593,850 employees in June 2010.

[c] Based on 2210356 employees in June 2010.

FECA and Retirement Age

Both FECA compensation and medical benefits are payable for the duration of a person's disability. There is no maximum duration of benefits and no maximum age at which benefits must be terminated. Beneficiaries who are eligible for CSRS or FERS retirement or disability annuities may chose to remain in the FECA program. Given the level of benefits, which can be as high as 75% of a worker's pre-disability wage; the annual cost-of-living adjustment to benefits; and the fact that FECA benefits are not taxed, in some cases the monthly FECA benefit is higher than what would be paid by a CSRS or FERS annuity. In addition, because FECA beneficiaries who are not working do not pay into either the Social Security system or the TSP, they may be unable to rely on these programs as a significant source of retirement income.

The Department of Labor reports that although less than 2% of new injury cases stay on the FECA rolls for more than two years, approximately 45,000 cases currently receive long-term disability benefits and 15,000, or one-third of these cases involve beneficiaries aged 66 or older.[20] The U.S. Postal Service Office of Inspector General reports that the FECA rolls include 9,554 postal workers aged 55 or older; 3,389 aged 65 or older; and 928 aged 80 or older, including one aged 99.[21]

The provision of FECA compensation benefits to workers after retirement age has changed during the history of the FECA program. Although FECA benefits have always been paid for the duration of disability, between 1949 and 1974, the administrator of the FECA program was required to review the amount of benefits paid to each beneficiary at the age of 70 and was authorized to reduce the amount of such benefits if it was determined that the beneficiary's wage-earning capacity had been reduced by his or her age, independent of his or her disability. This provision was repealed in 1974 with the Senate Committee on Labor and Public Welfare calling the reduction of benefits at the age of 70 "discriminatory."[22]

Policy Considerations

The question of whether FECA benefits should continue past retirement age depends somewhat on the intent of these benefits. If FECA disability benefits are intended solely to replace income lost by a worker because of an injury or illness, then one can reasonably argue that these benefits should stop at retirement age, when the worker would likely voluntarily stop working on his or her own, and thus no longer have wages to be replaced. It could be argued that the provision of FECA benefits for wage loss is analogous to the SSDI program, which stops paying benefits when a disabled beneficiary reaches retirement age. However, SSDI benefits automatically convert to Social Security retirement benefits at retirement age.

However, if FECA disability benefits are intended to provide some relief to the worker beyond wage replacement, such as providing additional money that might have been paid by an at-fault employer through the tort system or guaranteeing a certain minimum standard of living for a disabled worker, then stopping benefits at any age while the disability continues would violate this intent and deprive the beneficiary of deserved benefits.

Currently, 14 states and the District of Columbia place limitations on the duration of permanent total disability benefits under their workers' compensation systems. These limitations are in the form of a maximum number of weeks benefits may be paid, a termination of benefits at retirement or some other age, or a combination of both.[23] Federal workers' compensation benefits paid through the Longshore and Harbor Workers' Compensation Act are paid for the duration of disability or the life of the beneficiary.

FECA Benefit Levels

In general, FECA disability benefits are greater than those offered by state workers' compensation systems. For workers with traumatic injuries, FECA offers continuation of pay, at full salary, for the first 45 days. No state system currently provides any type of continuation of pay, absent the use of some form of sick or personal leave. Disability benefits under FECA are adjusted annually to reflect changes in the cost of living, a provision generally not found in state systems.

The maximum FECA benefit is based on 75% of the GS-15, Step 10 pay rate, without any locality adjustments whereas state maximums are generally based on state average wages or the worker's own pre-disability wage.[24] For 2013, the annual salary at GS-15, Step 10, is $129,517, whereas the average federal salary for the executive branch in December 2012 was $76,913.[25] Thus, the maximum FECA benefit under the current system is higher than it would be if the FECA system based its maximum benefit level on average wages as is the case in the majority of the states.

The FECA basic benefit rate for total disability is two-thirds of the worker's pre-disability wage. Currently, 36 states and the District of Columbia have total disability benefit rates that are set at this level.[26] Benefits under the federal Longshore and Harbor Workers' Compensation Act are also set at two-thirds of the pre-disability wage. New Hampshire's benefit rate is 60% of the worker's pre-disability wage.

Currently, four states have total disability benefit rates that are based on pre-disability or average wages and that exceed the two-thirds standard. In New Jersey and Oklahoma, benefits are paid at 70% of the worker's wage at the time of injury whereas benefits in Texas are based on 75% of the worker's average wage. In Ohio, benefits are paid at 72% of the pre-disability wage for the first 12 weeks, then are reduced to the standard two-thirds rate.

Six states—Alaska, Connecticut, Iowa, Maine, Michigan, and Rhode Island—base benefits on net, rather than gross wages. It is generally not possible to compare these benefits to FECA benefits because of differences in tax rates that affect net income. Three states—Georgia, Pennsylvania, and Washington—have systems in which there is no direct comparison to the FECA total disability benefit rate.

Because of the augmented compensation provision of the FECA program, beneficiaries with dependents, including spouses, may receive total disability benefits at a rate of 75% of their pre-disability wages. No state pays augmented compensation for dependents, and the 75% benefit rate is higher than that paid by any comparable state workers' compensation system. Currently, more than 70% of FECA beneficiaries are receiving augmented compensation, and thus benefits at the rate of 75% of their pre-disability wages.[27]

One comparison of the benefit levels of the FECA program with state workers' compensation programs involves the amount of disability benefits paid as a percentage of total program benefits. In 2010, disability benefits made up 49.9% of the total costs of benefits paid by state workers' compensation programs and 68.4% of total benefits paid by the FECA program.[28] If one assumes that the types of injuries faced by federal employees and workers in the private and non-federal public sectors are not significantly different and that medical costs are also similar, this difference can be attributed to the higher level of FECA disability benefits, especially for higher-wage workers, compared with those offered by state workers' compensation systems.[29]

Program Administration

Insurance

The administration of state workers' compensation systems and the provision of insurance and benefits differ significantly from the FECA program. The FECA program does not involve any form of private insurance or private third-party administration of claims or benefits. Essentially, each federal entity acts like a self-insured employer with OWCP in the role of claims and benefit manager.

State workers' compensation benefits are generally provided by private insurance, state insurance funds, or through self-insurance. All but four states—North Dakota, Ohio, Washington, and Wyoming—allow for private insurance. In Ohio and Washington, employers may either purchase insurance from the state fund or self-insure, whereas employers in North Dakota and Wyoming may not self-insure and must purchase coverage from the state fund. In 22 states, employers may purchase insurance from either a state fund or private carriers. All states except North Dakota and Wyoming allow self-insurance. Under the federal Longshore and Harbor Workers' Compensation Act, employers may purchase private insurance or self-insure.

Private insurance pays the majority of state workers' compensation benefits. In 2010, private insurers paid 56.7% of total state workers' compensation benefits whereas state funds paid 18.5% and self-insured firms paid 24.9%.[30] Thus, nearly three-quarters of all state workers' compensation benefits are paid through a system of third-party insurance rather than through the self-insurance model used by the FECA program.

Settlements

In 43 states and the District of Columbia, workers' compensation insurers or self-insured firms may enter into compromise and release settlements with claimants.[31] In these settlements, the insurer or firm agrees to pay the claimant lump-sum or periodic payment in exchange for being released from all future obligations under the claim. Compromise and release settlements are commonly used to avoid protracted disputes or litigation involving claims and are common in cases with potential for long-term payment of benefits. To accept a compromise and release settlement, the claimant generally must agree to forgo future benefits, which may be higher over his or her lifetime, in exchange for immediate payment. Insurers or firms must agree to forgo the possibility of lower future payments because of successfully controverting parts of a claim or the death, medical improvement, or return to work of the claimant, in exchange for clearing a claim off of their books with an immediate payment.

A 2010 study by the W.E. Upjohn Institute for Employment Research found that for 14 large states (California, Florida, Iowa, Illinois, Indiana, Louisiana, Massachusetts, Maryland, Michigan, North Carolina, Pennsylvania, Tennessee, Texas, and Wisconsin), for claims that originated between October 2003 and September 2004, and that had at least seven days of total lost work time, by March 2007, a median of 19% of these cases had been settled.[32]

Federal law does not provide for the settlement of FECA claims. Thus, the FECA program and FECA claimants are not able to take advantage of a tool used in approximately one-fifth of claims with the potential for long-term benefits, including the types of claims that are likely to result in beneficiaries receiving benefits well after retirement age.

Appendix A. FECA Scheduled Benefits

Table A-1. FECA Scheduled Benefits for Partial Disability Compensation

Loss of Use of Body System	Number of Weeks of Compensation
Scheduled benefits provided by statute [5 U.S.C. § 8107(c)]	
Arm	312
Leg	288
Hand	244
Foot	205
Eye	106
Thumb	75
First finger	46
Great toe	38
Second finger	30
Third finger	25
Toe other than great toe	16
Fourth finger	15
Loss of hearing in one ear	52
Loss of hearing in both ears	200
Scheduled benefits provided by regulation [20 C.F.R. § 10.404(a)]	
Breast	52
Kidney	156
Larynx	160
Lung	156
Penis	205
Testicle	52
Tongue	160
Ovary	52
Uterus or cervix	52
Vulva or vagina	52

Source: The Congressional Research Service from 5 U.S.C. § 8107(c) and 20 C.F.R. § 10.404(a).

Note: Compensation is equal to two-thirds of the pre-disability wage of a single employee or 75% of the pre-disability wage of an employee with dependents for the number of weeks indicated.

Appendix B. Legislative History of FECA

The FECA program has its origins in a law from the late 1800s that covered only the employees of a federal agency that has long since ceased to exist on its own. The modern FECA system has its roots in legislation enacted in 1916; many of the basic provisions of this original law, such as the basic rate of compensation, are still in effect today. Congress passed major amendments to the 1916 legislation in 1949, 1960, 1966, and most recently in 1974. Although these amendments made significant changes to the FECA program, the basic framework of the program endures as does the overall intent of Congress through the years to maintain a workers' compensation system for federal employees that is in line with the basic principles that have governed workers' compensation in this country for a century.

Limited Workers' Compensation for the United States Life Saving Service and Other Hazardous Federal Occupations

The first workers' compensation law for federal employees was enacted in 1882 and provided up to two years of salary to any member of the federal United States Life Saving Service disabled in the line of duty and two years of salary to his or her survivors in case of a line of duty death.[33] In 1908, Congress passed a more comprehensive workers' compensation law for federal employees engaged in certain hazardous occupations, such as laborers at federal manufacturing facilities and arsenals or workers at the construction of the Panama Canal. This law provided workers with up to one year of salary, after a 15-day waiting period, if disabled due to an employment-related injury and their survivors with up to a year of salary in case of death.

The 1882 and 1908 federal workers' compensation laws did not provide universal coverage for all federal employees. It is estimated that only one-fourth of the federal workforce was covered by the 1908 law, and the law was clearly designed only to provide coverage for what were seen to be the most hazardous jobs in the civil service.[34] President Theodore Roosevelt recognized this shortcoming of the law he would eventually sign. Before the 1908 law's passage, he called on Congress to pass a workers' compensation bill that would cover "all employees injured in the government service" and stated that the lack of such a comprehensive workers' compensation law was "a matter of humiliation to the nation."[35]

In addition to only covering a small portion of the federal workforce, the 1882 and 1908 laws did not provide for medical benefits for disabled workers, and the 1908 law only applied in cases of disability or death arising from injuries and not illnesses.

The Federal Employees' Compensation Act of 1916

President Woodrow Wilson signed the Federal Employees' Compensation Act, P.L. 64-267, into law on September 7, 1916, and in so doing extended the protections of the modern workers' compensation system to nearly all federal employees. This original FECA law remains the basis for the workers' compensation system for the federal civil service.

The FECA law provided coverage for nearly all civilian employees of the federal government injured or killed in line of duty. Coverage was not provided for occupational illnesses. The law provided full medical coverage for covered injuries to be provided by government physicians and hospitals or private medical services selected by the government. Disability compensation was provided, after a three-day waiting period, at a rate of two-thirds of the worker's wage for total disability, with adjustments for partial disabilities. Disability benefits were subject to minimum and maximum levels specified in the law and neither benefits nor these levels were subject to any cost-of-living or other annual adjustments. The survivors of an employee killed on the job were entitled to cash benefits based on the worker's wage and were also entitled to a benefit to help offset funeral costs.

The 1916 legislation created the Federal Employees' Compensation Commission, with three members appointed by the President with the advice and consent of the Senate, to administer the FECA program. Benefit and administrative costs associated with the program were paid out of the Employees' Compensation Fund created by the law and financed with permanently authorized appropriations.

Congressional Intent

Bringing the Federal System in Line with the States

Congress had several clear intentions when drafting the FECA program in 1916. One such intention was to bring the protections offered to federal employees in line with those being offered by a majority of the states at the time, with the House Judiciary Committee reporting that such state laws were "working with most excellent results."[36] In addition, the committee reported that the schedule of compensation for disability in FECA was "in line with the best precedents found in State compensation acts," especially those in Massachusetts, New York, and Ohio.[37]

Providing Coverage to All Federal Employees

An additional intention of Congress was to provide workers' compensation coverage to all federal employees regardless of occupation, thus correcting what was seen as a shortcoming of the 1908 act. The House Judiciary Committee's report on the 1916 FECA legislation criticizes the limited coverage of the 1908 law and states,

> The present law, in denying compensation to an injured employee if his occupation was not "hazardous" goes counter to the theory on which all compensation acts are based, viz, that the industry shall bear the burden of injuries caused by it.[38]

This criticism of the limited coverage provided by the 1908 act, and the intention of the FECA legislation to correct this shortcoming, was echoed by the FECA legislation's sponsor in the Senate, Senator George Sutherland. Senator Sutherland, in a Senate Judiciary Committee hearing on the legislation, stated,

> The theory upon which compensation laws are drawn is that you are to compensate for the injury, not for the risk that the man ran in bringing about the injury; and under modern thought there is no logical reason for making distinction between what is hazardous and nonhazardous employment.[39]

Senator Sutherland reinforced his point with a rather graphic example stating "the clerk who has his leg cut off in his work about a store is just as effectively deprived of his leg as if it was cut off by a machine."[40]

Major FECA Amendments

Congress has passed major amendments to the FECA program in 1949, 1960, 1966, and most recently in 1974. In addition, coverage for occupational illnesses was added to the FECA program in 1924 by P.L. 68-195.

1949 Amendments

The Federal Employees' Compensation Act Amendments of 1949, P.L. 81-357, brought about the first set of significant changes to the FECA program since its inception in 1916. The 1949 amendments, in the words of the House Committee on Education and Labor, sought to "modernize and liberalize" the

FECA program, which, according to the Senate Committee on Labor and Public Welfare, provided "only illusory security for most workers or their families."[41]

Increased FECA Coverage

The 1949 amendments expanded the scope of workers covered by the FECA program to include those classified as "officers" of the United States. The amendments also doubled the maximum disability benefit level, thus providing for a replacement of a larger portion of federal employee pay.

In addition to better meeting the goal of universal coverage of all employees, the inclusion of federal government officers was intended to provide FECA protections to previously excluded employees, such as Foreign Service Officers, who may serve in dangerous overseas areas. The increase in the maximum benefit level was necessary since, at the time, it was estimated by the Department of Labor (DOL) that 90% of FECA cases involved workers with wages that were essentially not covered by the program because of the low maximum benefit level.[42]

Increased FECA Benefits

Several provisions of the 1949 amendments effectively increased FECA benefits for workers and their survivors. The three-day waiting period for FECA disability compensation was eliminated in cases of disability lasting more than 21 days. A schedule of benefits for permanent partial disabilities was created for the first time, which permitted partial disability benefits to be paid without regard to actual impairment or wage loss. The elimination of the waiting period and creation of a benefits schedule were intended to bring the FECA program in line with state workers' compensation programs and the federal Longshore and Harbor Workers' Compensation Act program.[43]

The 1949 amendments provided for augmented compensation, in the amount of 8.33% of a workers' pre-disability wage, in cases in which an injured worker had at least one dependent. This augmented compensation, along with the standard compensation rate of two-thirds of the workers' wage, brought the level of FECA benefits for workers with dependents up to the current level of 75% of the worker's pre-disability wage. The benefit level for survivors was similarly increased. The intent of the augmented-compensation provision was to better ensure that disabled workers and the survivors of workers killed on the job could provide economically for their dependents. The two-thirds benefit level for dependents was criticized by the House and Senate committees that reported the bill as "not sufficient as to ensure reasonable economic security to a family of a deceased worker where there is a large family."[44] Similar concerns over the adequacy of the two-thirds benefit level were expressed at a House Committee on Education and Labor hearing on the 1949 amendments.[45]

Reduced Benefits at Age 70

Although the 1949 amendments generally increased the level of FECA benefits, the amendments also required the FECA administrator to review the amount of compensation paid to any person aged 70 or older. The administrator was provided the authority to reduce the amount of such benefits if it was determined that the worker's wage-earning capacity had been reduced because of age, independent of his or her disability. This provision was opposed by several representatives from federal employee organizations who testified before the House Education and Labor Committee. They testified that such a provision was inconsistent with the mandatory federal employee retirement age of 70, in place at the time, and could cause undue hardships to workers who, because of their disabilities, had not been able to reach their full-earning potential or who had reduced pensions because of many years of limited or no earnings.[46]

Provisions for Vocational Rehabilitation

The 1949 amendments permitted the FECA program administrator to send beneficiaries to receive vocational rehabilitation services at the government's expense. The amendments also created a special supplemental benefit for workers participating in vocational rehabilitation programs. These provisions were intended to improve the return-to-work prospects of FECA claimants, which, it was thought, would ultimately benefit both the employee through a return to earning wages and the government through a reduction in FECA-benefit costs.[47]

The Exclusive Remedy Rule

The 1949 amendments established that the FECA program would be the exclusive remedy against the federal government for federal workers with employment-related injuries, illnesses, and deaths. This provision prohibited employees from seeking to recover economic or non-economic damages from the government for injuries, illnesses, and deaths covered by FECA and brought the FECA program in line with one of the general principles of workers' compensation that was already written into the workers' compensation laws in the states.

When the FECA program was created, an exclusive remedy rule was seen as unnecessary because of the general prohibition against suits against the federal government. However, by 1949, three factors had combined to result in significant numbers of federal employees choosing to bring lawsuits against the federal government rather than file for FECA benefits. First, the passage after 1916 of laws, such as the Federal Tort Claims Act, which permitted some suits against the government.[48] Second, some injuries to federal employees occurred while they worked for government corporations subject to lawsuits. Finally, because FECA benefits are limited by statute to partial wage replacement and medical benefits, employees felt that they could secure greater financial benefits from the courts than from the FECA program.[49]

1960 Amendments

The Chargeback Process

The Federal Employees' Compensation Act Amendments of 1960, P.L. 86-767, created the chargeback process in which the Secretary of Labor is required to bill each federal agency for the costs of FECA benefits provided to their employees in the previous fiscal year so that these agencies may reimburse the Employees' Compensation Fund. In addition, these amendments required that government corporations also pay their "fair share" of FECA administrative costs to the government. The chargeback process was intended by Congress to "further the promotion of safety" among federal agencies by making the agencies ultimately responsible for the costs of injuries, illnesses, and deaths of their employees.[50]

1966 Amendments

The Federal Employees' Compensation Act Amendments of 1966, P.L. 89-488, made two significant changes to the FECA program. These changes continue to be in effect today.

Use of the GS Scale to Set Minimum and Maximum Benefit Levels

Prior to the enactment of the 1966 amendments, the maximum and minimum levels of FECA benefits were set by statute and not subject to any automatic adjustments. In 1966, FECA benefits were still subject to levels enacted as part of the 1949 amendments. According to the Senate Committee on Labor and Public Welfare, the statutory maximum provided for full benefits for more than 99% of claimants in 1949, but only 85% of claimants by 1966.[51] To address the difficulty inherent in using statutory changes to keep pace with the growth in federal employees' wages, the 1966 amendments provide for use of the general schedule (GS) scale as the basis for the maximum and minimum FECA benefit levels with the maximum level set at 75% of the highest rate of basic pay at the GS-15 level and the minimum level set at 75% of the lowest rate of basic pay at the GS-2 level.

Cost-of-Living Adjustment for Benefits

The 1966 amendments provided for an annual cost-of-living adjustment for FECA benefits.[52] This annual adjustment is a unique feature of the FECA program not found in other workers' compensation systems.

1974 Amendments

The Federal Employees' Compensation Act Amendments of 1974, P.L. 93-416, made three major changes to the FECA program. These three changes remain key elements of the program today.

Continuation of Pay

The 1974 amendments provided for up to 45 days of continuation of pay from a worker's employing agency in cases of traumatic injuries covered by FECA. During this period, an injured employee may receive his or her full pay rather than FECA compensation. Because continuation of pay is considered income rather than a benefit, it is subject to the federal income tax and is reduced by all standard payroll deductions.

Congress felt that 45 days of continuation of pay were needed because of the time it often took for FECA claims to be processed and compensation benefits to begin. In its report on the 1974 amendments, the Senate Committee on Labor and Public Welfare cited a General Accounting Office report that stated that the average processing time for FECA claims was between 49 and 70 days, a delay that the committee found "creates economic hardship on the injured employee and his or her family and causes difficult administrative problems for the Secretary of Labor and the employing agencies."[53]

Employee Choice of Physician

The 1974 amendments authorized employees to select their own treating physicians rather than use doctors employed or selected by the federal government. The right of employees to have free choice over who provides their medical care was one of the recommendations of the National Commission on State Workmen's Compensation Laws in 1972; this provision brought the FECA program in line with that recommendation as well as with some other workers' compensation systems.

Elimination of Reduced Benefits After Age 70

The 1974 amendments removed the provision, enacted as part of the 1949 amendments, requiring that FECA benefits be reviewed and permitting FECA benefits to be reduced after a claimant reached the age of 70 to account for the reduced earning capacity that may come with age independent of any disability. In its report on the 1974 amendments, the Senate Committee on Labor and Public Welfare provided the following justification for eliminating the reduced benefit provision:

> The Committee finds that such a review places an unnecessary burden on both the employees receiving compensation and the Secretary. Further, the fact that an employee reaches 70 has no bearing on his or her entitlement to benefits and is considered discriminatory in the Committee's opinion.[54]

Recent FECA Amendments

There have been no major amendments to the FECA program since 1974. However, the 109th and 110th Congresses did make changes to FECA that partially address two of the issues currently facing the program.

Change to the FECA Waiting Period for Postal Employees

Section 901 of the Postal Accountability and Enhancement Act, P.L. 109-435, changed the way the FECA three-day waiting period for compensation is applied to employees of the U.S. Postal Service (USPS). This provision requires that postal employees satisfy the three-day waiting period before the continuation of pay period can begin. All other federal employees continue to serve the three-day waiting period after the conclusion of the continuation of pay period and before FECA compensation benefits begin.

This provision was based on a recommendation of the President's Commission on the USPS. The commission's recommendation was part of a larger package of FECA reforms for postal employees intended to reduce the Postal Service's workers' compensation costs. Because of what the commission termed the "unique businesslike charter" of the Postal Service, the commission recommended that the service's workers' compensation system become more in line with the state workers' compensation systems that provide coverage for most private-sector businesses.[55]

Death Gratuity for Federal Employees Killed While Serving Alongside the Armed Forces

American military operations in Iraq and Afghanistan have been supported by an unprecedented number of civilian employees, some of whom are serving in hostile areas alongside the Armed Forces. These deployed civilian employees are covered by FECA, but concerns have been raised about the adequacy of FECA benefits for those injured or killed while serving in areas of combat, especially when compared with the benefits available to members of the Armed Forces from the Departments of Defense and Veterans Affairs.[56]

Section 1105 of the National Defense Authorization Act for Fiscal Year 2008, P.L. 110-181, provides for a death gratuity of up to $100,000 to be paid to the survivors of any federal employee, or employee of a non-appropriated fund instrumentality, who "dies of injuries incurred in connection with the employee's service with an Armed Force in a contingency operation." This death gratuity is paid in addition to the regular FECA compensation for survivors, but is offset by any other death gratuities paid by the federal government.

End Notes

[1] Department of Labor, Office of Workers' Compensation Programs, *Annual Report to Congress: FY2009*, Washington, DC, April 27, 2011, p. 7.

[2] Ibid., p. 15.

[3] United States Postal Service, Office of Inspector General, *Postal Service Workers' Compensation Program Audit Report*, Report Number HR-AR-11-007, Washington, DC, September 30, 2011, p. 8.

[4] Ishita Sengupta, Virginia Reno, and John F. Burton, Jr., *Workers' Compensation: Benefits, Coverage, and Costs, 2010*, National Academy of Social Insurance, Washington, DC, August 2012, p. 81. (Hereafter cited as Sengupta et al., 2012.) Direct administrative costs are OWCP's costs of administering the FECA program. Indirect administrative costs are for activities, such as investigations or legal support, outside of OWCP.

[5] Continuation of pay is defined in the regulations at 20 C.F.R. § 10(ee) as "a condition of the body caused by a specific event or incident, or series of events or incidents, within a single workday or shift." Certain groups, including federal jurors, Peace Corps volunteers, and Civil Air Patrol members, are not eligible for continuation of pay.

[6] The list of FECA scheduled benefits are provided in statute at 5 U.S.C. Section 8107(c) and in regulation at 20 C.F.R. Section 10.404(a).

[7] A copy of the current OWCP medical fee schedule can be found on the Department of Labor website at http://www.dol.gov/owcp/regs/feeschedule/fee.htm.

[8] Some federal employees, such as Foreign Service Officers or employees of non-appropriated fund instrumentalities, are covered by federal retirement systems other than CSRS or FERS. For additional information on the more than 30 types of federal retirement systems, see U.S. General Accounting Office, *Public Pensions: Summary of Federal Pension Plan Data*, GAO/AIMD-96-6, February 1996. For additional information on the FERS and CSRS, see CRS Report 98-810, *Federal Employees' Retirement System: Benefits and Financing*, by Katelin P. Isaacs.

[9] For additional information on the TSP, see CRS Report RL30387, *Federal Employees' Retirement System: The Role of the Thrift Savings Plan*, by Katelin P. Isaacs.

[10] The only payroll deductions taken from FECA benefits are for Federal Employee Health Benefits (FEHB) and basic, optional, and post-retirement basic life insurance if the employee is enrolled in these programs.

[11] P.L. 108-92.

[12] For additional information on disability retirement under CSRS and FERS, see CRS Report RS22838, *Disability Retirement for Federal Employees*, by Katelin P. Isaacs.

[13] 42 U.S.C. §424a.

[14] For additional information on the SSDI program, see CRS Report RL32279, *Primer on Disability Benefits: Social Security Disability Insurance (SSDI) and Supplemental Security Income (SSI)*, by Umar Moulta-Ali.

[15] Department of Labor, *FY 2014 Congressional Budget Justification: Office of Workers' Compensation Programs Overview*, April 2013, pp. 4-5.

[16] Department of Labor, Occupational Safety and Health Administration, *Federal Injury and Illness Statistics for Fiscal Year 2012*, http://www.osha.gov/dep/fap/statistics

[17] Department of Labor, Office of Workers' Compensation Programs, *FY2010 End of Year LPD Report for All Government*, http://www.dol.gov/owcp/dfec/share/lpd/FY20104 thQtr/AllGovernment.htm.

[18] The total number of lost production days is calculated by CRS based on June 2010 employment data compiled by the Occupational Safety and Health Administration (OSHA) from various sources and posted on its website at http://www.osha.gov/dep/fap/statistics and on end-of-fiscal year injury data reported by the Department of Labor on its website at http://www.dol.gov/owcp/dfec/share /lpd/FY20104 thQtr/AllGovernment.htm. Because the number of federal employees fluctuates throughout the year, and because no one agency of the federal government collects data on employment in the executive, legislative, and judicial branches of the government, the calculated number of total lost production days must be treated as an estimate. The estimated number of lost work years is calculated based on 260 work days in a work year.

[19] Department of Labor, Office of Workers' Compensation Programs, *Annual Report to Congress: FY2009*, Washington, DC, April 27, 2011, p. 11. A chargeback year runs from July 1 to June 30.

[20] U.S. Congress, Senate Committee on Homeland Security and Governmental Affairs, Subcommittee on Oversight of Government Management, the Federal Workforce, and the District of Columbia, *Examining the Federal Workers' Compensation Program for Injured Employees*, 112th Cong., 1st sess., July 26, 2011 (statement of Gary Steinberg, Acting Director, Office of Workers' Compensation Programs).

[21] U.S. Postal Service Office of Inspector General, *Postal Service Workers' Compensation Program: Audit Report*, Report Number HR-AR-11-007, September 30, 2011, p. 1.

[22] S.Rept. 93-1081, p. 7.

[23] Sengupta et al., 2012, pp. 87-95.

[24] The maximum benefit is only paid to workers with wages at the high end of the GS scale or above, at the time of injury.

[25] Information on the GS-15 salary rate taken from the website of the Office of Personnel Management (OPM) at http://www.opm.gov/policy. Information on average federal salary taken form the OPM FedScope system online at http://www.fedscope.opm.gov/.

[26] Sengupta et al., 2012, pp. 87-95.

[27] U.S. Congress, Senate Committee on Homeland Security and Governmental Affairs, Subcommittee on Oversight of Government Management, the Federal Workforce, and the District of Columbia, *Examining the Federal Workers' Compensation Program for Injured Employees*, 112th Cong., 1st sess., July 26, 2011 (statement of Gary Steinberg, Acting Director, Office of Workers' Compensation Programs).

[28] Sengupta et al., 2012, pp. 24-25.

[29] This conclusion is supported by Sengupta et al. who state "The share of benefits for medical care is lower than in most state programs because federal cash benefits, particularly for higher-wage workers, replace a larger share of pre-injury wages than is the case in most state programs" (Sengupta et al., 2012, p. 80).

[30] Sengupta et al., 2012, pp. 24-25.

[31] Peter S. Barth, *Compromise and Release Settlements in Workers' Compensation: Final Report*, W.E. Upjohn Institute for Employment Research, report prepared for the State of Washington, Department of Labor and Industries, December 21, 2010, pp. 44-45, http://research.upjohn.org/reports/178/.

[32] Ibid., p. 43.

[33] Act of May 4, 1882, ch. 117, 22 Stat. 55 (1882). In 1915 the United States Life Saving Service was merged with the Revenue Cutter Service to form the United States Coast Guard.

[34] Willis J. Nordlund, "The Federal Employees' Compensation Act," *Monthly Labor Review*, September 1991, p. 5. (Hereafter cited as Nordlund 1991.)

[35] U.S. Congress, House Committee on Education and Labor, Subcommittee on Safety and Compensation, *Amendments to Federal Employees' Compensation Act*, hearings on H.R. 1196 and other bills to amend the Federal Employees' Compensation Act, 86th Cong., 2nd sess., February 10, 23, 24 and March 8, 23, 24, 1960 (Washington: GPO, 1960), p. 124.

[36] U.S. Congress, House Committee on the Judiciary, *Compensation of Government Employees Suffering Injuries While on Duty*, report to accompany H.R. 15316, 64th Cong., 2nd sess., May 11, 1916, H. Rept. 64-678 (Washington: GPO, 1916), p. 7.

[37] Ibid., p. 9.

[38] Ibid., p. 8.

[39] U.S. Congress, Senate Committee on the Judiciary, *Accident Compensation to Government Employees*, hearing on S. 2846, 64th Cong., 1st sess., February 26, 1916 (Washington: GPO, 1916), p. 27.

[40] Ibid.

[41] U.S. Congress, House Committee on Education and Labor, *Amendments to Federal Employees' Compensation Act*, report to accompany H.R. 3141, 81st Cong., 1st sess., June 6, 1949, H. Rept. 81-729 (Washington: GPO, 1949), p. 23, hereafter cited as H.Rept. 81-729; and U.S. Congress, Senate Labor and Public Welfare, *Amendments to Federal Employees' Compensation Act*, report to accompany H.R. 3141, 81st Cong., 1st sess., August 4, 1949, S.Rept. 81-836 (Washington: GPO, 1949), p. 29, hereafter cited as S.Rept. 81-836.

[42] Nordlund 1991, p. 10.

[43] The Longshore and Harbor Workers' Compensation Act Program was created in 1927. For additional information on the Longshore and Harbor Workers' Compensation Act, see CRS Report R41506, *The Longshore and Harbor Workers' Compensation Act (LHWCA): Overview of Workers' Compensation for Certain Private-Sector Maritime Workers*, by Scott Szymendera.

[44] H.Rept. 81-279, p. 11; and S.Rept. 81-836, p. 20.

[45] U.S. Congress, House Committee on Education and Labor, Special Subcommittee, *Federal Employees' Compensation Act Amendments of 1949*, hearing on H.R. 3191 and companion bills, 81st Cong., 1st sess., April 11-13 and May 2, 1949.

[46] Ibid.

[47] H.Rept. 81-279, p. 16; and S.Rept. 81-836, p. 24.

[48] For additional information on the Federal Tort Claims Act, see CRS Report 95-717, *Federal Tort Claims Act (FTCA)*, by Vivian S. Chu.

[49] H.Rept. 81-279, p. 14; and S.Rept. 81-836, p. 23.

[50] U.S. Congress, House Committee on Education and Labor, *Federal Employees' Compensation Act Amendments of 1960*, report to accompany H.R. 12383, 86th Cong., 2nd sess., June 2, 1960, H.Rept. 86-1743 (Washington: GPO, 1960), p. 3; and U.S. Congress, Senate Committee on Labor and Public Welfare, *Federal Employees' Compensation Act Amendments of 1960*, report to accompany H.R. 12383, 86th Cong., 2nd sess., August 27, 1960, S.Rept. 86-1924 (Washington: GPO, 1960), p. 3.

[51] U.S. Congress, Senate Committee on Labor and Public Welfare, *Federal Employees' Compensation Act Amendments of 1966*, report to accompany H.R. 10721, 89th Cong., 2nd sess., June 16, 1966, S.Rept. 89-1285, p. 3.

[52] The current cost-of-living adjustment is made each year on March 1 and is based on changes in the Consumer Price Index for Urban Wage Earners and Clerical Workers (CPI-W; all items-United States city average) as measured in December of each year.

[53] U.S. Congress, Senate Committee on Labor and Public Welfare, *Federal Employees' Compensation Act of 1970*, report to accompany H.R. 13871, 93rd Cong., 2nd sess., August 8, 1974, S.Rept. 93-1081 (Washington: GPO, 1974), pp. 3-4, hereafter cited as S.Rept. 93-1081; and U.S. General Accounting Office, *Need for a Faster Way to Pay Compensation Claims to Disabled Federal Employees*, B-157593, November 21, 1973, p. 1.

[54] S.Rept. 93-1081, p. 7.

[55] President's Commission on the United States Postal Service, *Embracing the Future: Making the Tough Choices to Preserve Universal Mail Service*, Report of the President's Commission on the United States Postal Service, July 31, 2003, p. 134.

[56] See, for example, U.S. Congress, House Committee on Oversight and Government Reform, Subcommittee on Federal Workforce, Post Office, and the District of Columbia, *A Call to Arms: A Review of Benefits for Deployed Federal Employees*, hearing, 111th Cong., 1st sess., September 16, 2009; and U.S. Congress, Senate Committee on Homeland Security and Governmental Affairs, Subcommittee on Oversight of Government Management, the Federal Workforce, and the District of Columbia, *Deployed Federal Civilians: Advancing Security and Opportunity in Afghanistan*, hearing, 111th Cong., 2nd sess., April 14, 2010.

INDEX

D

E

J

L

M

N

O

P

T

U

V

W